TILL I END MY SONG

Halfpenny Bridge, Lechlade

TILL I END MY SONG

BY

ROBERT GIBBINGS

With wood engravings by the author

NEW YORK: E. P. DUTTON & CO., INC.: 1957

TO

RALPH BEEDHAM

Sweete Themmes runne softly, till I end my Song.
SPENSER, *Prothalamion*.

CHAPTER ONE

I WAS TIRED and hungry on my last evening in London, and my flat was in chaos after the exertions of the furniture removers. 'It's early,' I said to myself, 'but there are places in Soho where people are often a bit irregular in their meal times. I'll go along there and see if I can find strength for the morrow's journey.'

'Yes, sir, you wish to relax and enjoy your food, sir,' said the venerable waiter to whom eventually I was committed. 'Is that chair wide enough for you, sir?

There's nothing like comfort for digestion, sir. Comfort and the right wine, sir, alter the whole complexion of a meal, sir.' He stepped aside to fetch a wine list.

In whatever other ways he encouraged me to relax, he gave little prompting to be silent. Rarely did the old man pass my table without a comment, answerable or otherwise, upon the state of the world, the catering trade, or other subjects. After we had discovered some acquaintances in common he became confidential.

'That man over there with the girl in black, sir, he's unhappily married, sir. Gives him a chance to take a different girl out every other night, sir. Everything in life has its compensations, sir.'

He was busy with other tables while I drank my coffee—'In my job, sir, you need to be blind of one eye and deaf of one ear, sir'—and I had to wait some time for my bill. When at last he laid it before me he sighed as if apologizing for the price. 'Things aren't the same nowadays, sir. They've changed, sir, and they'll go on changing, and the only consolation for a gentleman of your age, sir, is that you're on your way out, sir.'

'I *am* on my way out,' I told him, 'out of London to-morrow to live in the country, in a cottage about the size and shape of a thatched beehive.'

'If I may say so, sir, in a manner of speaking, sir, I hope you'll find it well stored with honey, sir.'

I tried to tell him that the cottage was beside the Thames, in a quiet village in Berkshire, but he wasn't listening.

'Honey, sir, is good for the liver, sir, and if you are

inclined to generosity of the figure it's better for you than sugar, sir.'

I told him that my liver was in good working order but that I would remember his advice. Then he came closer and spoke to me almost in a whisper. 'A word before you leave, sir. If ever you should want a valet, sir, you'll find him here, sir. I'd be proud.'

By the same hour next day I was sitting before an open fire in my newly acquired cottage. I listened for the sound of traffic but there was none. I listened for sounds of the country but there were none. Only one moo of one cow throughout the evening. All I could hear was silence. Earlier I had stood awhile in the garden. The pear-tree on my lawn was tipped with crimson, the elms beyond my boundary hedge were fringed with gold. Though it was early October, a precociously minded sparrow was playing with a feather. The two tall lime-trees that overshadowed my gate seemed friendly, neighbourly, with none of the impersonal aloofness of city trees. Everywhere was the quiet of hidden growth, and only two minutes' walk from my gate lay one of the loveliest backwaters of the Thames.

Two minutes, indeed. It could only have been that if I had worn blinkers. Along the Green Lane I went next morning, looking at the medlar fruit and tangle of wistaria boughs that topped a high Cotswold wall, looking still higher at a flock of lapwings that moved like a dark smudge across the sky. Then through a wicket gate and down a steep path to a clear streamlet running over yellow gravel. A gardener was cutting flower stakes from a nearby clump of bamboos.

'St Anthony's Well,' he said, with a jerk of his thumb towards the stream. 'Many moons ago the old people would come and bathe their eyes if they were weak. It would cure them if they had the faith. Not many have it now, not in these parts. They have it in my country, though. I'm a Celt from the Cambrian Hills.'

The water poured into a long moat-like pond whose surface was tapestried with the amber of fallen leaves on the dark and light greens of duckweed and starwort. Bordering the pond, on the further side, was a wilderness of water scrub from which rose islands of crimson dogwood.

'In May the place is white with lilies,' said the Celt. 'Some calls them Summer Snowflakes, some calls them

Loddon Lilies. They grows very thick by the Loddon river, down towards Henley.'

He asked me where I lived and I told him that I had come to live in Long Wittenham.

'That's an old cottage you've got,' he said. 'Five hundred years old, I'd say. 'Course they've done a bit to it of late. You ask young Roley Ayres that lived there before the war. He used to say, "If a rat comes in under our door, there's room for a dog to follow it."'

I left him to his bamboos and made my way along a grass path, passing dry ditches that must soon be full of water, passing a willow-tree among whose bare branches the neat cup of a reed warbler's nest was still securely woven into place. Blue tits and marsh tits flashed and flitted among yellow leaves. Beyond a foam of grey and purple reed plumes I found the river.

When, about the middle of the nineteenth century, the Thames Conservancy dug a canal rather more than half a mile in length above Clifton Hampden, they cut off a loop of the Thames that was to become one of the pleasantest backwaters on the river. From where I stood I could see before me a wide crescentic pool whose low banks on the far side spread away into wide sunlit pastures, whose high banks shadowed with elms on my right sent their reflections deep into the water. Sixty and a few miles since much of the water sprang from the earth; another hundred to flow before it would mingle with the sea. Little traffic on the back-water, the only boat in sight that of a fisherman dozing hopefully. There are no salmon nowadays and few trout, yet at the beginning of the last century salmon fry were so plentiful in the lower reaches of the river that they were trapped in weirs of brushwood and carried away by the cart-load as food for pigs and manure for the land. It would be a poor pig to-day that depended on salmon fry for its provender.

Immediately opposite to where I stood the bank was steep and in places undercut by the current. The roots of an elm, the nearest to the river of several, were protruding from the bare earth. One more flood and there'll be one less tree, I thought. In the March that followed my prophecy proved true, for hardly had the melted snows passed on their way from the western hills than many a cubic yard of soil subsided into the stream. With it fell the sap-heavy timbers of that elm. The silt passed on but the tree remained to sprout its leaves above stream level and to gather debris that, weir-like, deflected the current from further erosion of the bank.

CHAPTER TWO

TO BUILD a house is exciting but not as exciting as to build a studio, for the house when completed is an end in itself whereas the studio is but a means to an end, a beginning. Shelter and comfort and love and hot baths are well and enjoyable in their place; but an easel with a bare canvas in a bare room can hold dreams beyond the telling.

My only regret during the construction of the new building was that so much living soil had to be buried as if dead. The same thought often occurs to me when I see country lanes being turned into arterial roads, orchards uprooted so that lorries can bring apples from elsewhere.

First of all came coarse gravel, foundation for the concrete floor, and no sooner was the first barrow-load spilled on the site than I forgot the gooseberry bushes and cabbages that had been torn up, for here were fossil remains of creatures who had lived many million years ago when this same valley was under water and the climate was tropical. Of broken bivalve shells, oysters and scallops, and fragments of coral, there were quantities; numerous too were the pencil-like cones whose originals were the 'bones' of cuttle-fish corresponding to those white pumice-like disks which to-day are fed to canaries.

'Thunder-stones we calls 'em hereabouts—comes down with the 'ail,' said the builder's apprentice; and I remembered the belief among many primitive peoples in Indonesia, Africa, and elsewhere that the pre-historic stone axes which they find are 'thunder-stones' that have fallen from the sky during storms. Among the aborigines of Arnhemland in north Australia there is a legend of a Lightning man, Mamaragan by name, who during the monsoons travels in the thunderclouds and with his stone axe strikes at trees and people on the ground. When I mentioned this parallel to a lady long resident in Wittenham, adding that among those primitive peoples the stones were frequently used as charms against illness both in men and cattle, she said: 'But I remember an old man who worked as gardener at the vicarage here—he collected those stones and ground them up as medicine. He reckoned they were a cure for all kinds of stomach complaints.'

While the mason was putting the last smoothing touches to the cement floor, an onlooker remarked to me: 'What you want now is the imprint of a film star's foot.' And the words were hardly out of his mouth when a robin alighted on a nearby wheelbarrow and from there hopped across the wet concrete.

'We've got the footprints of a singer, anyway,' said the mason. Those prints still decorate my floor.

As I watched the scantlings of sides and roof being articulated and the skeleton of the building taking form, I could visualize finished canvases that were one day to hang on the cool grey walls. I could see too the

unfinished ones that would stand on a narrow breast-
high shelf, awaiting further contemplation. There
would be a wider shelf also, perhaps for figurines in
clay, almost certainly to hold my Yoruba twins,
fertility figures which had been brought to me from
Nigeria—they should be valuable in a studio, if controlled. Where shavings were heaped in a corner
would stand a two-bushel osier basket such as farmers
use in the potato fields and orchards. I reckoned that
waste paper thrown from anywhere in the room could
hardly miss that mark. And of course pinned to the
walls would be drawings, notes from past ideas, hints
for new ones.

The first visitor to the finished studio was small—a
ladybird, saffron in colour with nine black spots. It
was when I was lighting the initiatory fire in the stove
that I noticed it walking across the floor, which to
one of such lowly vision must have seemed a vast
desert of rock. When I picked it up it feigned dead,
as many other small creatures do when touched; but
soon enough after I had put it on the window-sill it
opened its wings and disappeared. Of the four
thousand known British beetles the ladybird is surely
the most charming: useful too in its destruction of
green fly. I often wonder how ants, who shepherd
the aphis for the honeydew they secrete, regard the
ladybird and its larvae who feed directly upon them.

My next visitor to the studio was an old man named
Simeon Kimpton to whom I had been introduced when
I visited my old friend Harry Chambers, landlord of the
Plough. He brought me some bottles of beer that I

had ordered from Harry, and it seemed only reasonable
that we should open one of them.

'Nice bit of glass you've got,' he said, looking at the
big windows and the top light, 'but you've got it on
wrong side for sun.'

'It's for painting, not for plants,' I told him.

He put his mug down on the table and went up to a
still life of fruit that hung on the wall.

'Wonnerful year for tomatoes it's been,' he remarked; 'never known such a year—not one of mine
but ripened.' He moved on to a painting I had recently finished of Shillingford Bridge. 'That's where
I lost a big chub last season—in that bed o' reeds
near the bridge,' he said.

Then he came to a standstill in front of a group of
nude female figures. For some moments he stood in
silence. 'Lush!' was his only comment.

'I knowed an artist once,' he said as he picked up his
mug again, 'lived other side of Warborough. A nice
man he was, by name of Hill, Caleb Hill.

'A queer thing happened about him. He was
living in the village with his wife and two kids, a
bit younger than him she was, and he was a popular
man—everyone liked him. I was living there too at
the time. And one night I was up at the local, must
'a' been 'bout half past nine, a dark wet night, and I
was talking to Fred Fitten. He was reserve champion
milker at Smithfield that year, and he were telling me
about the show. ''Tractors like war tanks,'' he said,
''you'd walk round 'em to see where the guns was
hidden''—he'd been in the army a bit—''and the

prize heifer of the show," he said, "fed on whisky by-products!" 'Twas when he were telling me how she was owned by a man in a distillery that Jack Fossey, the landlord, hears the telephone and goes out. A few moments later he puts his head through the hatch from the private bar and he beckons to me to come in to him. "Could you take a message to Caleb Hill?" he said. "You'll be passing his house."

'"I could," I says, "when I'm going home."

'"That's too late," he says in a kind of a low voice. "It's from the hospital in Reading," he says; "his wife's took bad and wants to see him."

'"That's funny," I says, "must 'a' been an accident, saw her meself tea time. She were well enough then."

'"Better hurry, I think," says Jack.

'So I went along and I knocked at the door and Mrs Hill herself opened it. I felt a bit awkward at that.

'"I'm glad to see you, Ma'am," I says, "I'm glad to see you looking so well, Ma'am," I says, "but do you think I could have a word with the master?"

'She seemed a bit surprised at the way I spoke, but she said no more than "Stand inside out of the wet and I'll send him down to you."

'Caleb comes down the stairs and into the hall. "It's a bad night outside," he says.

'"It is," I says, "and I'm feared I be bringing bad news. I don't understand it," I says, "but a message came in just now from Reading to Jack Fossey and it says will you go as quick as you can to the 'ospital 'cause your wife is bad and wants to see you."

'He didn't say nothing but I could see he was shook.

"I'll come with you in a moment," he said as I was backing to the door. "I must find a taxi."

"'I'll get Ted Bristow for you," I said; "he's at home to-night."

'He thanked me and I fetched the car.

'He give me a lift the half-mile to my cottage, and he hardly spoke a word till I was leaving him.

"'Simeon," he said, "me and you's been good friends since ever I come to this village. I'd like," he said, "if this could be a private affair between us."

'That was a long time ago and I've never said a word to another. But he's dead now, and you is a writer and you is a painter, and they do say that artists is very sensible people.'

Simeon left me, but before he had crunched many steps on the loose gravel that I had just laid he turned and came back.

'I forgot to tell you,' he said, 'that 'bout six months after that night Mr Hill and his wife, as we knew her, left the village, and we was all right sorry, for they were a proper decent pair. 'Twas in Ted Bristow's taxi, the same as before, that they went in to Reading to the station.

"'A funny thing," said Ted to me that night in the pub, "a funny thing this morning," he said, "but just as we gets to Reading Mr Hill calls out to me: 'Stop a moment at the Register Office,' he says. 'I'll leave the children with you; we won't be more'n a few minutes,' he says, and he and his wife got out. They was a good quarter of an hour inside, and they nearly missed their train."

'"Getting birth certificates for the children perhaps," I said; "they'd maybe be wanting 'em for the
new schools."

'"Why," said Ted, "I never thought o' that."

'But I knew 'twas another kind of certificate they
was after. An' I never let on not a word.'

Harry Chambers of whom I have spoken was the last
of many generations of his family to be landlords at the
Plough. A hundred and fifty years they'd been there.
'Long enough,' said Harry to me. 'I'm leaving soon.'
And he did and I was sorry.

The first time we'd met was when I came to the
village to visit A. E. Coppard soon after he had moved
from his wooden hut in the Henley woods to a sixteenth-century brick and timbered house in Long
Wittenham. That was about the year 1927, and I used
often to come over from the other end of Berkshire to
see him, for not only was I publishing and illustrating
many of his stories at the Golden Cockerel but he was
guiding my financial footsteps in that same small
private press. Little did I think then as we sun-bathed
in his garden that the tumbledown bit of wattle and
daub and thatch on the other side of his hedge would
one day be my own snug habitat.

It was for his *Count Stefan*, published in 1928, that
I engraved his portrait as a frontispiece. Curiously
enough it remains not only the one successful likeness
that I have ever achieved but was, he used to say, the
only successful one among the many attempts by artists
who specialized in portraiture. Though his features

were strong and clear-cut as a gipsy's, their mobility gave them a quality of elusiveness.

'A *nice* man, Coppard,' said Harry. 'I liked to see him come into the bar. He wasn't young then, must have been getting on for fifty, but he'd have the football boots on and he'd be talking about the Saturday game as if the Houses of Parliament depended on it.'

'I remember him buying a new pair when he was sixty,' I said, 'and swearing he'd wear them out.'

'And when he heard anyone tell a good story he'd begin to twist that long black forelock of his—remember that habit he had? And then he'd get the boys singing. Folk-songs he liked. He'd sing them himself, picked up from all over the place. "Augustus John brought that from Ireland," he'd say, or somebody else heard that in Suffolk. But *Billy Boy* was his favourite. "Where have you been all the day, my Billy boy?" and finishing up with his Nancy tickling his fancy. Yes, he went to live in Suffolk after. Believe he's living there still—and he'd be young yet by *his* standards.'

In January 1957, little more than a year later, Coppard died at the age of seventy-nine. The best of his stories, wrote the *Manchester Guardian*, are 'instinct with his vivid interest in human beings, his sense of the beauty and the sorrow of the earth, and of a heaven that is both magic and compassion.'

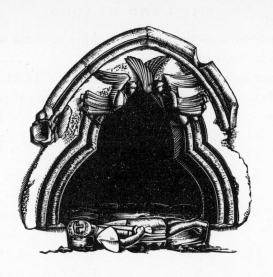

CHAPTER THREE

Almost everything in Long Wittenham carries
the patina of age or ancestry. Scarcely a
house in the village that does not show
ancient beams and generations of thatch.
Parts of the cross which stands on the green outside my
gate date from the first half of the seventh century
when St Birinus, Bishop of Dorchester, converted to
Christianity the pagans of Witta's ham, the settlement
of Witta the Saxon. Rising land to the south of my
garden is known as Saxon's Heath, and there not only
two hundred skeletons of those pre-Norman settlers
have been found but many of their bronze implements
of war. The atmosphere is such that when one dark
night a small gnome-like boy came to my door and,
holding out six coppers in the palm of his hand, said:
'Will you give me a silver sixpence for these?' I began

15

to wonder what spell he was about to weave in his subterranean home.

The church is built on the site of a pre-Christian burial ground and in all probability replaces an earlier church of timber: its chancel arch dates from the beginning of the twelfth century. Other parts of the building, including a 'priest's door' and a piscina for the washing of holy vessels, are but a century later. The piscina is remarkable in that along its lower edge and in front of the basin is the sculptured figure of a knight in armour, a crusader with legs crossed, measuring no more than twenty-five inches in length: it is said to be the smallest sculptured monument in England. The leaden font, brought from Rouen in the twelfth century and having as embellishment the figures of thirty archbishops with their right hands raised in blessing, would not have escaped Cromwellian iconoclasm but that a timely encasement of wood was made to hide the images. Only in 1830 when the sheltering timbers were removed did those prelates see the light of day again. Until recently a copy of Foxe's *Book of Martyrs* was kept chained to the lectern in the old manner, and therein one can read of John French of this village who suffered greatly for his faith. In the garden of the heavily thatched and timbered house known as 'French's,' which stands across the road from my cottage, is the ancient barn in which he is said to have been immured.

Also in the vicar's keeping is a prayer book dated 1707 in which, following immediately after the Thanksgiving Service for Queen Anne's accession, is the service to be used 'At the Healing.'

'. . . Then shall the infirm Persons, one by one, be presented to the Queen upon their Knees, and as every one is presented, and while the Queen is laying Her Hands upon them, and putting the Gold about their Necks, the Chaplain that officiates, turning himself to Her Majesty, shall say these words following: "God give a Blessing to this Work; and grant that *these* sick *Persons*, on whom the Queen *lays* Her Hands, may recover, thro' Jesus Christ our Lord."'

I had always thought that a touch, without ceremony, was all that was needed from the royal fingers, but here and from subsequent study I learned that in the majority of cases an elaborate ritual accompanied the act. First and most important, it was ascertained by the sergeant surgeons to the throne whether or not the case was curable—this, quite reasonably, following a precedent set by the Roman Emperor Vespasian, A.D. 69–79, who when in Alexandria, being entreated by a man in the crowd to touch his afflicted eyes with spittle, inquired first of his physicians if the case were curable. John Evelyn tells us that on 28th March 1684, 'there was so great a concourse of people with their children to be touched for the Evil, that six or seven were crushed to death by pressing at the chirurgeon's door for tickets.' In Traill and Man's *Social England* we read that at that time 'the Ceremony was one of the spectacles that the gay world went to see. Charles II sat in state in the Banqueting House, attended by the surgeons, the chaplains, and the Lord Chamberlain. The opening prayers and the Gospel having been read, the children were brought up in order to the steps of the throne, where kneeling they were stroked on either cheek by the king's hands, the chaplain saying over each, "He put His Hands on them and healed them." When they had all been touched, they came up again in the same order, and each had a white ribbon with a medal of angel-gold hanging from it, put round the neck by the king. Then followed the Epistle, special prayers (in the old Prayer Books) and the Benediction.'

The medal of angel-gold mentioned here was a substitute for the Angel Noble, a gold coin first minted by Edward IV in 1465 and having as its device the archangel Michael destroying the dragon. This was the coin presented to all supplicants when 'touched' by the king. It was last coined in the reign of Charles I, after which small medals bearing the same device were given instead.

Through hardly more than a 'priest's door' one passes from the grounds of the church into the grounds of the manor house, once belonging to Abingdon Abbey. Here stands the tall pigeon cote of timbers and zigzag brickwork from which 1,200 pairs of birds went forth to feed on tenants' corn; here are still the fish-ponds whence fat bream and chub were taken to comfort fasting clergy. At that time many a man who did not fast was hungry for the like.

The manor or demesne of Long Wittenham goes back in history beyond the Norman Conquest, belonging at one time to Ealdgyth, daughter of Godwine, Earl of Essex, who in 1045 married Edward the Confessor. Thence it passed to William the Conqueror, who bestowed it upon his cousin the Lord of Longueville

in Normandy, who had furnished thirty ships for the invasion of England. So many earls have there been among the overlords of the village that at one time it was known as Earl's Wittenham. To-day the adjective 'long' is descriptive of the single street that runs east and west, hardly more than a stone's throw from the river, edged on either side by houses for the most part of wattle and daub, crooked beams, and cranky brickwork. It wasn't long after I came to live in my cottage that I discovered that one of its walls consisted of mud, straw, and cow-dung held in place by a few erratic beams. When some supporting ivy fell the mud fell too, and overnight I acquired a window that let in the first rays of dawn.

So far I have discovered no hoard of coin or treasure behind my crumblous plaster, but among the beams of an old barn near by there was recently found a copy of *The Times* for 9th November 1796, a date when that majestic newspaper was but eleven years old. Only a single sheet then, folded to make four pages, it has since on occasion reached as many as thirty-two. Of that early issue the first and the last pages were given up entirely to advertisements, not the paltry few lines that we find in the personal column of to-day but fine generous measures of space, inches deep.

Pride of place at the top of the first column on page 1 is given to 'Extraordinary Large Reptile.—The Curious are hereby informed that there is now to be seen the largest and most beautiful RATTLE-SNAKE ever imported to this Kingdom. . . . Its bite is attended with immediate dissolution.'

In the second column a gentleman wishes to purchase 'a Place in either the Navy, Admiralty, Victualling, or Excise Offices, or Custom-House.' In column three is advertised 'An Asylum of Genius, where complete justice will be done to Literary Works, and Money *occasionally* advanced to the Authors themselves . . .' (the italics are mine). Then attention is drawn to tonic tinctures, analeptic pills, and cardiac remedies. Finally in the same column is recommended 'To the Female Sex.—The never-failing excellence of Mr Edward's Globular Herbal Nipple Cases.'

On page 2 is announced the 'resignation of George Washington, Esq., of his situation of President of the United States of America,' and on the final page are offered quantities of cinnamon, cloves, and other spices, 'being part of the Cargoes of sundry Ships

bound from Amsterdam to Spain.' The French had
driven the English out of Holland in 1794; the English
had driven the Dutch out of India in 1795; Spain was
allied to France and Holland in 1796. Small wonder
that cargoes had been changing hands on the high seas.

It was in 1850 that Mr Ingram Shrimpton, a printer
living in Long Wittenham, sent a party of six young
craftsmen, including two of his own sons, to New
Zealand, to establish the *Lyttelton Times*. Taking their
equipment with them they sailed in the *Charlotte Jane*,
730 tons, one of the fleet of four ships that carried close
on eight hundred colonists to the newly founded
Settlement of Canterbury. True pioneers they were.
Their first job, the printing of an Import Customs form,
was completed before the roof of their one-storeyed
workshop had been put on; for six months after that
calico took the place of glass in their windows. The
journal lasted until 1935, and not the least of many
exciting incidents in its career was a visit to the
editorial offices by Dame Nellie Melba who, furious
that a critic had written adversely of her singing,
demanded that he should be publicly thrashed. The
critic agreed to this on condition that she did the
thrashing herself, that it should take place in a public
hall, and that he would receive the whole of the takings.
The case did not proceed.

An aged man cutting grass on the village green outside my gate enlightened me as to the purpose of the
small brick shelter which stands there near to the cross.

'Why, that were the house for fire engine,' he said. 'But it's no more than ten foot by six,' I remarked.

'Big enough for *our* fire engine,' he said. 'Three wheels and a tank. Six men worked the 'andles, three on one side, three on t'other. All the villagers carried the buckets, kind of a chain it was, the men passed 'em along full o' water and the women passed 'em back empty. Now let me see, last time we used engine must 'a' been in nineteen 'undred and nine—Widow Beasley's house, a spark from the chimney set the thatch alight. There was two other houses alongside and they caught alight too. The wind were very high and it blew the flames. It was Widow Hewitt lived in one of them, and a man by name of Weston, George Weston, a shepherd, he lived in the other. All three was burnt to the ground, the houses I mean, 'twas the thatch that took 'em. Yes, we worked hard that day, water from every well in the village, but we couldn't stop it. It cracked the glass and it melted the lead in Mr Bodkin's windows near by, Sir Archibald he is since, but we didn't let it go no further. Leather buckets we had, a couple of gallons each, bought off some old man-o'-war, they say. Real strong 'ide, and copper rivets. There's a few of 'em about in village still—they got "L.W." painted on 'em in white, for "Long Wittenham."'

That evening I was talking to my neighbour, Dick Gower.

'What became of the old fire engine?' I asked him.

'I bought it,' he said. 'Bought it for a quid, no one else bid higher than ten bob. Why, the hose was worth more than that. And I sold the gun-metal for seven pound ten.'

'Nothing of it all left now?' I inquired.

'Only the door of the valve box, with the maker's name and the date on it.'

I asked him if I could see it.

'I'll give it to you,' he said. 'I'll pop it through the hedge in the morning.'

True to his word, he brought it along next day. 'Wm Cole, Lambeth, 1779'—light and dark lettering on a pale apple-green panel of teak. 'There you are,' he said, 'you keep it.'

And there it stands to-day in a corner of the studio, beside my own little printing press.

CHAPTER FOUR

ONDAY the 16th January seemed to be the turn of the year. Looking from my window that morning I saw at the edge of the lawn three small white flecks, the first snowdrops; and then looking upward I saw, in the elms, rooks bowing to each other beside their past season's nests. When just then the postman brought me a letter from a lady of seventy-six asking if I would take her to a dance, I felt that spring had indeed arrived.

It was a day of light. By the river everything shone luminous, unsubstantial. When I tried to lift a fallen willow branch, it was a surprise to find that it had weight. The surface of the water was a mirror adding illusion to unreality: only a floating twig betrayed the current. The dense curtain of reed plumes was like a

24

froth of milk into which ochreous earths had been stirred. There was silence save for faint murmurs from the distant weir. Lapwings shimmered but made no sound as they passed overhead in scores.

It was only as I began to move up-stream towards Appleford that a robin's notes retrieved reality. Snipe too rising solitary or in wisps from the water's edge disturbed the calm with their protesting cries, and mallard broke the stillness of both air and water as they scuttered and rose from last year's rushes.

Then as I watched the twitchings of the soil where a mole was working, there came to my ears, like chords in a tone poem of Sibelius, the long rhythmic beat of heavy wings, and looking up I saw close-knit in majestic flight six white swans following the course of the river.

At Appleford—famous for onions, 'grows there as free as carrots'—I found the Black Horse where I had left it in 1939. That was a favourite haunt of John Faulkner, the jockey who rode his first winner when he was eight, was still in the saddle at seventy, had thirty-two children, and died at the age of 104.

Set in the wall of the house beside the door was a china plaque which portrayed an artist in eighteenth-century dress, holding in one hand a palette and in the other a tankard of beer. The figure seemed a little unsteady on his legs. Indoors I noticed the same device on the labels of the beer bottles.

'"The Drunken Artist," trade mark of the firm. This is a Morland house,' said Mr Hervey, the proprietor.

'Why choose an artist?' I asked.

'There was a Morland, an artist,' said Mr Hervey. 'George, I think his name was—some relation of the firm. He used to paint horses and pigs. He used to paint inn signs too. They say his price for a sign was all the gin he could drink while he was doing the job.'

'I reckon he wouldn't 'urry with his work,' chuckled an old man sitting by the fire.

'The prices for his work to-day would buy a lot of gin,' I said. 'There's one of his paintings—a horse in a stable—in the National Gallery in London.'

'He liked his gin and he liked his horses. They say he was a good jockey too,' said Mr Hervey.

'Like old Faulkner,' I suggested.

'He died younger—about forty he was, I believe. The only thing he wouldn't drink was tea—he said it made his hand shake.'

When I got up to go and inquired if I could follow the river to Sutton Courtenay, the old man got up too.

'It's awkward by the river,' he said, 'better keep to road. I'll come with you, might as well walk it on a fine day. If Bert calls,' he instructed the landlord, 'tell him I don't need a lift to-day. Tell him I gone walking with a gentleman. Just over a mile,' he said to me as we set out. 'I goes there regular once a week to visit Agnes, that's my sister. There's only the two of us left now, the first and the last, Agnes and me. Ten of us there was, all the others is gone. Eighty-seven Agnes will be come Christmas, and active as a hen. ''What's eighty-seven?'' she says. ''Look at Martha Pye in the churchyard, south of the chancel— a hundred and seventeen. And Reuben,'' she says to

me, "I'll beat that or I'll die." That's her little bit
of fun. Nothing she likes better 'n a joke. "I'd
rather a laugh than a shilling," she says, and mind you
she used to say that when a bob was worth twelve
coppers.'

We passed one of the fish ponds that belonged
formerly to Abingdon Abbey, and then along a level
unfenced road through the wide-spreading arable valley.
Three corn stacks close to the road had on their sum-
mits plaited ornaments of straw, an aeroplane on one
and a bird on each of the others.

'Dollies they call 'em,' said Reuben. 'Mr Napper,
that's the farmer whose man does 'em. Proper artist
that chap is. Last year they had four ricks and he put a
traction engine made o' straw on each of them. 'Twas
to celebrate the race they have at Appleford each year—
all the old tractions polished up and scoursing round
the field, and the half of 'em boiling over. Dangerous
it is, with the safety-valves all wired up an' a flywheel
like to blow off.'

We crossed a small stream, a deep-cut boundary
between two many-acred fields. The grey plumes of
its reeds showing above the bare tillage on either side
marked its course across the valley—one streak of
wildness in such ordered husbandry.

O let them be left, wildness and wet;
Long live the weeds and the wilderness yet.

Gerard Manley Hopkins's lines came into my mind,
but my companion was talking about education.

'You can always learn something in a pub,' he said.

'I always say a pub is a good school—if you don't get too abbreviated. Why, I never knowed before to-day that the "Drunken Artist" was a real man. I never knowed till a week ago last Friday that a sparrer 'as twice as many bones in 'is neck as a giraffe. 'Twas in the Barley Mow and Jack Soames comes in with a crick in 'is neck—'is head was turned crooked with it. "Thank God I'm not a giraffe," he says, "or I'd be looking behind me."

'"You'd be worse off if you was a sparrer," says a feller who was standing by the bar. "A giraffe has only seven bones in 'is neck, a sparrer has fourteen," he says. Some kind of a perfessor from Oxford, I think he was.

'Yes, and last Saturday in the Black 'Orse, old Matt Harman was talking about diarrhoea. "Acorns is the cure for that," he said. "Grind a few of 'em up small and drink 'em with milk," he said, "and you'll be right in an hour. Better'n all the brandy in the world," he said, "and you want no opener after."

'But I wish I'd been edicated proper,' went on Reuben. 'I wish I'd been brought up a gent—a real old-style gent, some of them fellows as sets themselves up to-day is just ridicure, plain ridicure.'

He was silent for a while, as if meditating. Then as I was about to remark on a heron in a sandpit pool, motionless as a mooring-post, he spoke again.

'But I 'ad me day once,' he said. 'In Alexandria it was, in Egypt, during the first war. I was batman to a captain, regular Army and real posh—the shine I put on 'is boots, he could shave in 'em. He was down to sing

in a concert one night, regimental show and brass 'ats
coming along.   Last minute his throat went bad, could
'ardly speak.   "Andrews," he said to me—well,
'twas 'ardly more 'n a whisper—"Andrews," he said,
"you got to take my duty to-night.   Put on my togs,"
he said, "you've laid 'em out for me but put 'em on
yourself, and you go and sing for me," he said.   "Any
song you like," he said.

'So I put on his evenin' togs and they fitted me a
treat.   And I acted like an officer and didn't they clap
—why, I brought the 'ouse down!'

'What songs did you sing?' I asked.

'Well,' he said, 'I gave 'em "The long, long trail"
—good chorus that—and then for an encore I gave 'em
"Lily of Laguna."   That got 'em proper.   You should
'ave 'eard 'em roar the last line!'   He stopped in the
middle of the road and, with chest thrown out, let me
have it: 'My lily and my ro—se!'

At the entrance to Sutton Courtenay we parted
company, he to continue his way to the other end of
the village where his sister lived and I to take the foot-
path that led to the pools and their many weirs.   There
had been rain in the west and the water was galumphing
through those sluices with a joy unbounded.   Slowly
and calmly it moved in the main stream above, so slowly
that one might have swum in it with ease.   But of a
sudden as it came within the influence of the fall it
wavered, and next moment in fierce abandon a trio of
rapids had arched their backs and plunged through the
gates.   Then in an instant they were froth, white froth
in a welter, prancing, curvetting, rushing ahead,

curling back. The patterns that the intercepting currents made in the wide pool beyond the foam were like the patterns wrought on shield and in missal by the ancient Celts, long swinging curves with sudden unexpected backward sweeps. Even the fallen willow leaves caught in the eddies seemed echoes from those early designs.

I was once asked the significance of these figurings and  I could only answer that they seemed perfectly to express the Celtic temperament, dreaming spirals of thought returning on their own tracks to launch forth again on curling waves of adventure, the seemingly haphazard accents corresponding to the inconsequent digressions of humour in an Irishman's conversation.

But just then my thoughts of the Gaels were momentary, for looking beyond the turmoil of waters I saw, floating in a quiet pool under willows, my six swans of the morning. Then, as they passed over, the music of their wings had reminded me of Tuonela, the murky Hades of Finnish mythology; but here now were birds that might have been the fleecy cloud-like Apsaras of the Indian heaven. My late friend, the poet Edward Powys Mathers, once likened love to birds over moving water under trees. Here was delight bright as the sparkle of love in many eyes, tintinnabulous, tuned to sing.

CHAPTER FIVE

Y LILY and my Rose! Isn't it a strange thing that though the prettier names of our wild flowers are in constant use as expressions of endearment, we seldom use the less mellifluous ones when referring to people not quite to our liking. We all have our Lilies, our Roses, our Daisies, and our Violets, in thought if not in name—in France even a 'little cabbage' is a term of affection—but few seek in the hedgerows for epithets of an opposite nature. How comforting it would be if sometimes we could refer to a grumpy old man as a Mugwort, to one who had 'done us wrong' as a Black Horehound, to one that had acted meanly to us as a Weasel Snout. Gallantry forbids more than one reference to the ladies, but what a solace it would be to a heckled male if just once in a while he could refer to the object of his devotion as 'that bit of old Fleabane.'

With the mildness in the air my thoughts had been running on assurances of spring—the crocuses that would soon be putting a variegated stipple on my lawn, the aconites already spreading their pale gold under the chestnut-tree in Little Wittenham churchyard, the Christmas roses in sheltered nooks straightening their curling bud stalks, and the purple flecks of aubretias on dividing walls—when, without a single hint of its sinister intention, came 'a frost, a killing frost.' Overnight the world was transformed: windows were muffled with frost, everything outside of them was

starched with ice.   The tip of every twig was sunk in
a shining nodule: willows by the river shone like
chandeliers, with lustres hanging on every spray.
Under them, due to a falling of the river level, dry stalks
of willowherb and loosestrife each supported a shining
inflorescence, every bloom fantastic as an orchid.   At
Sutton Courtenay I found the piers of the locks draped
in grey transparent shawls with long icicle fringes.   No
warmth in those shawls, no warmth in the wind that
blew half-frozen spray against them, no warmth in
what you could put on, only in what you could put in:
I repaired to the Fish, adjacent to where I had parted
from Reuben a few days earlier.

Indoors a Negro with canary coloured scarf about his
throat stood by the counter.   He smiled as the landlord
poured him a glass of Jamaica rum.   'In my country
we make a good medicine for this weather,' he said.

'Sixteen bob a gallon when I was there,' I remarked.

'Why, sir, you been in my country?' he asked with
delight.

'Only a few days,' I said.   'But I'd like to go back.'

'Have you, sir, by any chance sufficient money for
the two of us to return together?' he asked.

'It's too expensive to live there nowadays,' I said.

'That is the great difficulty in my country to-day, sir.
It is too expensive for the rich man to live richly, it is
too expensive for the poor man to live poorly.'

'Herefordshire I come from,' said the landlord.
'Leominster—the loveliest town in the county.'

'"Trip a trap a trencher, say the bells of Lemster,"'
I quoted.

'Where did you learn that?' he asked.

'In the Wye valley, years ago,' I said.

'Better fish there than you get here,' he suggested.

'I know,' I answered. 'I had a friend in the valley, a poacher.'

A corner of an eye twitched. 'Have this one on me,' he said.

We were all set to forget the pewter-coloured day outside. Our Negro friend had introduced himself as Zechariah Wilson.

'What do you think of that barracuda sign over the door?' I asked him.

'Pike,' interpolated the landlord.

'*Becune* we call him in West Indies,' said Zechariah.

'A big pike will run to forty pounds in this country,' said the landlord.

'They go fifty in Ireland,' I said.

'A *becune* goes sixty pound in Jamaica. More dangerous than a shark,' said Zechariah.

'They call the pike "the knight of the sad face" in France,' I said.

'They'll attack an Englishman before a Frenchman,' said Zechariah. 'Englishman eats more meat, his flesh smells stronger in the water.'

The hooting of a motor horn outside reminded me of a van that was to give me a lift towards home. An icy blast through the half-opened door confirmed that it was waiting.

'Mind if we go by Clifton Hampden?' said Mickey, the driver. 'Got a plumber on board to deliver.'

Peeps of the river showed sheets of broken jagged

ice, like steel plates after an explosion. Around the trunks of the willow-trees, a foot above the water level, were thick frills of ice, like the tutus of ballet dancers.

'I once heard tell,' said Mickey, 'that the Dutch Fleet was captured by cavalry when the sea was frozen over. I'd believe it now.'

We put our passenger down by a house from whose thatched eaves icicles hung in curtains; then crossing the long brick bridge whose existence just then seemed redundant we steered a course for Wittenham.

'Drop me at the far end of the village,' I asked, 'I've got to collect some eggs before I go home.'

Mercy Ward came from her goose pen to greet me. She had in her hand a bunch of feathers from the wing of one of her Chinese geese.

'I have to pull them,' she explained, 'to keep the old girls from flying.'

The feathers were the first six primaries of a wing, and she held them as though they were playing cards. It was impossible not to notice the variation in outline of one plume from another. The first feather had a narrow line of web, uniform in width for its whole length, forming the leading edge of the wing; but aft of the quill the web, broad at the base, was sharply indented midway in its length and then tapered to its tip. The second feather, which lay partly overlapping the first, was likewise indented and tapered but on both sides of the quill, its outline suggesting a poignard exquisitely fashioned for fell purposes. The forward web of number three was akin to that of number two, but its hinder margin was a sweet unbroken curve.

Numbers four, five, and six echoed in less marked degrees the same features.

The wings of many other birds are similarly fashioned, the spaces thus created between the feathers allowing the airstream to pass through and prevent the formation of impeding eddies.   Such gaps are clearly defined in

the wings of buzzards and other birds of prey who need a power of quick manœuvre when pursuing their quarry: they occur also in the short broad wings of game birds that frequent thick coverts and need a similar ability when speeding among trees.   Plain for all to see are the fingered wing tips of rooks as they perform their aerial evolutions.   Slotting in the wings of aeroplanes is an application of the same principle, gaps that allow the airstream to pass without the formation of eddies.

I often wonder why among the multitude of human beings who *must* collect something there are not more who collect feathers, who in their walks by stream or hedgerow do not glean the plumelets dropped from wing or tail or rump.   Among our home birds the specula of mallard and teal are known to all for their iridescent purples and greens; the blue-and-white bars of a jay's wing are only too well appreciated by dressers of headgear; the dazzle of the kingfisher makes even the most ruthless destroyer hold his hand.   But there is sheen and patterned loveliness too in the plumage of starling or sparrow, magpie or finch, and splendour in the white primaries of a swan.

Meal-worms, that's what's needed for robins.   I had a feeling that I owed something to the author of those footprints on my studio floor.   So along I went to the pet shop in Oxford market, expecting to be served by some wizened human being whose features had taken on the expression of the mice, guinea pigs, or marmosets that occupied his cages.   Instead there smiled at me a girl who would have shone in a beauty parlour.   Canaries sang around us, tropical birds twittered, and I had to ask this owner of manicured fingers to serve me with meal-worms.

'Oh yes,' she said, 'one and eight an ounce.'   She slipped her hand into a bin of squirming larvae as tenderly as if she were adjusting a baby's bonnet and brought forth a palmful of writhing maggots.

'Bran and wholemeal flour suits them for breeding?' I asked.

'Yes,' she said, 'and put a couple of cloves in the box, too—they like the scent.'

As time passed and it became known in the village that I cherished a brood of these worms, fishermen would come with perforated tins, asking me if I could spare a handful of bait; and thus I became a maggot merchant. But let it be said that in my dealings I never charged a penny. It would have been a come-down on my Income Tax Return if after 'By royalties' I had had to add 'By maggots.' There would surely have been questions asked. Soon after I took over the Golden Cockerel Press in 1924 I published Brantôme's *Lives of Gallant Ladies*, and in due course showed on my balance sheet the abbreviated title of the book and its profits: 'By Gallant Ladies—£220.' The Inspector of Taxes in an early reply requested that I would explain this particular item. It went to my heart to disillusion him.

CHAPTER SIX

I MMEDIATELY opposite to Appleford, on the Oxford-shire side of the river, there is a small plot of land which belongs to Berkshire. It is a little triangular spinney, about half the size of a tennis-court, and it is clearly marked on the Ordnance maps.

'Why that speck of Berks on the north side of the river?' I asked Mr Hervey in the Black Horse.

'Well,' he said, 'they say that one time there was a body found there on the bank, a man who'd been drowned, and no one in Oxfordshire would do any-thing about it—didn't want the bother of the inquest and all that kind of thing. They said that anyway he was a Berkshire man. So the Berks people said: "We'll deal with him then, but that bit of land will be ours ever after."'

When I spoke of this in the hearing of Harry Cooper, long a resident of Wittenham, he said to me: 'If you turn up the road towards Brightwell and walk to the top of Sire Hill, no more than a mile from your door, you'll come to a bit of land there called Dead Man's Piece. That used to belong to Wittenham parish, now it belongs to Brightwell, and that's because a body was found there—an old tramp he was or maybe a gipsy. "He's nothing to do with us," says Witten-ham. "All right," says Brightwell, "we'll bury him," and ever since then the land is part of Brightwell parish.'

Another long-time resident of Wittenham told me

that when as a young man he lived near Standlake, higher up the river, his father's uncle decided that *he* would be the man to end once and for all an argument about a right of way.

'"When I die," he said to his sons, "you put me on the door and carry me by that path across the field to the churchyard. Don't go round by the road," he said; "put me on the door, the same door that carried my father and his father before him—it comes off the hinges very light—and carry me by that path. Of course," he says, "if I die in the field put me on a hurdle—it's easier to handle than a door—but make sure it's that path. We have the right to it," he says, "and no man, newcomer or oldcomer, has any right to touch it." And no man has put a plough near it since.'

In the Journal of the Folk Lore Society it is recorded that 'on 19th October 1948 the body of a drowned man was refused passage through a toll-gate by the gate-keeper of Lincoln College, Oxford, on the grounds that such a proceeding would immediately create a right of way. Eventually the police had to lift the body over a wall.' And that in Oxford, city of light and learning, less than ten years ago.

While on this sobering subject, I must tell of one Martin Cole who lived at Newbridge, as a friend of his told the tale to me.

'Fisherman? We used to think he'd soon be growing scales. "Give me a rod to hold," he said when he was dying. Them was his last words. And when we come to read his will, there was all his gear to his son—his reels, his nets, his stool, and all the rest.

Not a word of his money—'course he didn't have much. "And cremate me," he says, "cremate me and throw me into the river by the second gate." That was his favourite corner for fishing—the second gate up from the bridge.

'The floods was out and 'twas raining hard the day we took that pot o' ashes along the towpath, and there was some that said: "The first gate is far enough, *he* won't know," but me and his other special pals we said, "No, we got to go to second gate like he said, even if we drown as we go. He wouldn't float quiet," we said, "if we throw him in here." So we carried the ashes up and we spread 'em gently where the current would carry 'em out from the bank.'

CHAPTER SEVEN

THE HARD weather continued. Now was the time when, as Nicholas Breton wrote in his *Twelve Moneths* (1626): 'Fishermen have a cold trade, and travellers a foule journey: the Cook room is not the worst place in the Ship, and the Shepheard hath a bleake seat on the Mountaine.'

I had hoped that within a few days the robin who had picked bread crumbs from within inches of my feet would be eating from my hand. I remembered that Lord Grey had said, 'Robins will risk their lives for meal-worms,' and that the whole process of taming these birds may take only two or three days in hard weather. In this case, not a bit of it: the colder the weather the more aloof and unfriendly that particular bird became. Whereas in December and early January it would sit in the elder-bush close to my door, ready at any moment to chirp a few notes if I came near, ready at the first sign of a crumb to come hopping towards me, now it was disdainful, ready only to turn its back, slip through the hedge, and disappear. The meal-worms that I put down were gulped by thrushes and blackbirds before ever it returned.

The reason for this display of temperament soon became apparent. Never in their existence had these birds found so much food spread before them. The village lawns, swept of snow, were white with bread; prunus and laburnum trees which decorated gardens were garnished with bacon rinds and scraps of fat;

coco-nuts hung from eaves and trellises like bells on pagodas. The abundance was such that after I had scraped a path and scattered crushed corn and bird-seed, the greater part of what I threw remained untouched until after nightfall. Only then, and by the small creatures of darkness, were my efforts appreciated. As to chunks of bread dropped into my garden by birds passing overhead, Elijah in his cave was not better supplied by the ravens.

Outside the village it was not so easy. Where a heron rose on the frosted river-bank there lay a cluster of black and brown barred feathers attached to a fragment of bone, the tail of a snipe, and scattered around were the pale breast feathers of the same bird. Harassed by cold or weak from long flight, it had been pounced upon by the omnivorous heron and swallowed whole, long beak, legs and all, save only the tuft of the tail and the fragments of down.

The cold persisted, light snowfalls alternating with gleams of sunshine by day and spells of black frost at night. Ploughed fields were striated with the snow that lay luminous within the furrows of dark soil. Everywhere the trident footprints of birds, and late in the evening when the moon rose towards fullness, scraped on the untrodden snow of a pathway the inscription 'Harry loves Hetty.' Elsewhere there were eighteen degrees of frost.

Then as rapidly as the temperatures had fallen they rose again. The snow melted overnight and almost in a matter of hours the garden was lit by crocuses, bright as candles in the night. And with the hardness out

of the ground and the worms nearer to the surface, the thrushes raced to and fro on the frost-broken tilth, pecking and pulling and swallowing.

Worms, hundreds of thousands of them in our garden soil, travelling in their tunnels, passing the earth through their bodies as they go, coming to the surface only at night to seek a mate or find a leaf that suits their palate.   Willow and iris leaves they like, fir needles too and the cups of beech mast, but strangely fastidious they scorn others that to a non-worm might seem more succulent.

In their mating there is a wonderful tenseness as with heads towards tails they lie together, parallel, moment-arily fused by a secretion from their skin.   On mild moist nights by the light of a torch they may be seen on any lawn, taut and motionless, as each receives sperm from the other, for they are hermaphrodite.   The eggs are not fertilized at this mating; only later, as each worm wriggles backwards through the outer membrane of its girdle—the swollen band conspicuous about its middle—are the ova and spermatozoa shed by separate ducts into that capsule of skin.   There, in the discarded cocoon, the two elements meet and there the young develop.

Gilbert White, writing in 1770, remarked that 'earth-worms though in appearance a small and des-picable link in the chain of Nature, yet, if lost, would make a lamentable chasm,' and without them the earth 'would soon become cold, hard-bound, and void of fermentation.'   He goes on to say that 'a good mono-graphy of worms would afford much entertainment and information at the same time, and would open a large and new field in natural history.'   Could the hints which he thought 'proper to throw out in order to set the inquisitive and discerning to work' have been the germ from which just a century later Charles Darwin brought to birth his treatise, *Formation of Vegetable Mould through the Action of Worms*?

But neither Gilbert White nor Charles Darwin spoke of the delicate colours ranging from shell pink and lilac to deepest heliotrope that suffuse these tapering creatures when seen on the surface at night; and it was not until 23rd March, when at four o'clock in the morning I woke to my sixty-seventh birthday, that I came to realize that what we are accustomed to see as squirming and lustre-lacking individuals when thrown up by the spade in daylight could be static as the sphinx, shining, and vivid as buds of crimson polyanthus among their own green leaves. The early morning airs were mellow, there had been light rain, and I was wide awake. I crept barefoot downstairs and on to the lawn sequined by the rain. Elsewhere I have written of my emotions when for the first time I wandered on the coral reefs of Bermuda, twenty feet below the surface of the sea; here in my own garden was a similar excitement. Flower-beds were streaked with these spun-glass tubes of colour; snake-like, claret-coloured forms bedecked the grass.

I have often envied creatures of the night for the privacy and freedom in which they live, wandering in their own time through our cherished preserves without let or hindrance, laughing to themselves at the thought of our un-private daylight existences. Slugs were out that night, too, gliding with dignity; and as I heard afterwards an otter was active in the backwater, catching an eight-pound barbel, the greater part of whose body it left upon the bank.

Slugs may not compete with Birds of Paradise in conjuring up ideas of romance in human minds, yet in their modest way they have moments that are enviable. *Limax maximus*, one of the large black variety from which delicate human fingers recoil, finds its mate on the leaf of a tree and follows it until the two, meeting and exuding a thread of slime, drop together by its means into mid air. There, suspended only by that filament which shines silver as the moon, they accomplish their desires.

I asked a man who was pollarding willows in the water meadows if he had ever seen anything of the kind.

'Never seen the like o' that,' he said. 'But last year I seen two grass snakes in that near thorn-bush. The two of them was twisted together like ropes, and they was all tangled up in the branches, and when I touched 'em with a stick they didn't move. I reckon they was mating.'

CHAPTER EIGHT

'MY LORD, what a morning!' All the spiri-
tuals that Dvořák echoed from the New
World are re-echoed in the streams that
flow into the upper Thames on a bright
spring day. Coln, Leach, Windrush, Evenlode, and
many a smaller brook, bringing their clear waters
south from the Cotswold hills, twisting and turning
upon themselves as they flow as if to make a joke of
their course.

On a day in March that might have been in May I
browsed beside the Coln where it passes through the
town of Fairford. Fayre-ford indeed. From the old
mill weirs and sluices the water ripples and glides
sparkling over gravel whose every pebble if rare would
be a jewel. Its course is cushioned with bright
cresses; darker strands of weed wave like idling trout.

White-nosed coots and red-nosed moorhens cross and recross from reeds to sedge. Above the mill swans and Canada geese sail like galleons among the fleets of smaller craft, the mallard with heads brighter than the grass and the tufted ducks blacker and whiter than ink on paper and more gay than ever a song that was printed.

Oh, the brightness of spring sunshine, on the tattered golds of marsh land, on the young greens of stream-side meadows, on the pink of fat pigs, on the rose of old brick walls. Colour dances, even on the roads, to the music of the wind.

Moving into the town, I inquired about conveyances to Lechlade of an elderly lady who with a full shopping bag beside her was sitting in a bus shelter.

'You haven't long to wait now,' she said; 'there'll be one along in about an hour and a half.'

So to fill those brief moments I dropped in to the nearby churchyard. The church itself, with its four-teenth- and fifteenth-century glass, I had visited many times before, but this was a day to put joy even into tombstones. I wandered among the cherubs. Never had I seen so many angels' heads in such small compass. But why did they have to frown? Surely to goodness *they* ought to be happy. Lichen had turned the hair of many of them to gold, and by the same means a few had been gilded on the nose, but there wasn't one of them that didn't pout, not one that showed the least effort to sing. You'd think they were dominated by the winged skull that glowers from a sarcophagus dated 1662. No encouragement to glory at all, I thought, as with clouds breaking the clear sky above my head I made my way back to the shelter in the square.

Arriving at Lechlade I called at the New Inn. 'Could you give me a cup of tea?' I asked David Fitzgerald who greeted me.

''Twould be a pity if we couldn't,' he answered.

'You can't get away with only a cup of tea,' said his sister Sheila who came in a few moments later. 'Hasn't my horse won to-day?'

So the clouds that had gathered over the tombstones seemed to disperse, and as twilight fell the evening grew brighter and brighter and the stars came out two by two.

At the foot of the New Inn garden runs the Thames, and but a few hops of a foot to the west from that garden is the bridge which provided the frontispiece to this book, and only one jump with both feet from that bridge is Peter Ford's boatyard.

'Peter is in the tea-room,' said Gordon Hawke, his partner, from under a punt upturned on trestles on the slipway.

Early in the year to be open, I thought, as I turned the handle and went in.

Tea-room indeed! It wasn't tables with white cloths that I saw before me but skiffs—two doubles looking twice the size they'd be on the water. Peter was standing beside one of them with a brush in his hand.

'Yes,' he said, 'scrub and scrape and paint through the winter. Four coats of varnish on the clean wood.

Floor-boards, gratings, back rests, stretchers, oars, and paddles, they've all got to be done. Of course some need more than others.'

The tea-room had the appearance of a heraldic arsenal. A score of shining rudders rested against one wall looking like medieval shields, dozens of oars like jousting lances leaned against another wall, paddles lay about like clubs.

'Things may be quiet in the summer if the weather's bad,' said Peter, 'but there's no quiet in a boatyard in the winter.'

Back at the New Inn, James Baxter, partner with Miss Fitzgerald, was talking to a stranger who had a face not unlike one of the two greyhounds that he held on a leash. David was behind the bar, smiling at everyone as he always does, and chatting to a small middle-aged man in a moleskin cap who was sitting in the seat close up to the bar. James was being polite to the stranger, answering his questions about the hunting horns, the coach horns, the racing spurs, and the other sporting trophies that decorated the walls.

'And not as much as the collar of one hound among them,' said the stranger disparagingly; 'have you never followed coursing?'

'Here's the lad for hares,' said David, pointing to the man with the moleskin cap. 'He runs 'em down in his bare feet.'

There was a moment's silence.

'It's a Labrador I've got,' said the little man. 'I puts snares along the hedges and fences, and then I ties

a tin with a few stones in it to the dog's collar and I lets
him loose for a run. He puts up every hare in the
fields. I got seventeen of 'em in one night.'

With hardly a good night, the man with the hounds
went out.

'What are you doing, David, driving custom away?'
asked James Baxter.

'Wouldn't it make you laugh?' said David.

CHAPTER NINE

FOR SUNDAY the 8th of April the Wittenham and Clifton Hampden Piscatorial Society had made an assignment with the Oxford Anglers' Association to remove two tons of coarse fish from the waters of the Windrush in the vicinity of Burford and transfer them, live, to the Wittenham backwater. Twelve pounds ten shillings a ton the anglers were to be paid, though the piscatorials were to be responsible for the carriage.

'Electrocution, that's how it's done,' said Dick Gower. 'They run a current of electricity through the water and the fish gets a shock that stuns 'em. It doesn't do 'em any harm, just knocks 'em out so they float down-stream and then the boys are ready with the nets. You'd better come along and see,' he said, 'it's good fun. There's a spare seat in Jack Pritchard's car. The Taynton flats, above Burford—they'll be starting around nine o'clock Sunday morning.'

We reached the scene at ten o'clock, to find about twoscore of men and boys gathered by the narrow stream. Though the waters in their loopings and twistings had travelled some thirty miles from their source and drawn into themselves the rills of many Cotswold valleys, yet the two banks were scarcely twenty feet apart and the water seemed no more than a foot in depth. A lorry with an electric generator on board stood in the meadow, and from it a cable stretched through the grass to a bamboo rod bound with copper wire that lay across the river and was controlled with ropes by men on either bank. Eight men with long-handled nets were scooping up the stunned fish and flicking them on to the banks.

'Mind your head!' called a voice as a friendly hand pushed me from the trajectory of a four-pound pike. A small boy rushed to the spot where it had fallen, picked up its inert form, and carried it in both hands to a water-filled dustbin. Chub were dropping on to the grass quicker than the boys and the lookers-on could gather them into the bins, roach too and an occasional perch. It surprised me that there was scarcely a fish that would not have been worth the catching: I had expected to see minnows, gudgeon, dace coming up, thick as plankton in a whale's belly; but no, hardly a tiddler.

'That's the value of pike in a river,' said a stout man with a waterproof cap; 'keeps the numbers down and the size up.'

The electrified rod was moving down-stream and the dustbins were growing heavy to carry when boxes with slotted sides came floating down the river and the catches were transferred.

'But where are the trout?' I asked. 'I've only seen three. I thought this was a trout river.'

'They want to make it one,' he answered. 'That's why they're letting us have the coarse fish. They stocked it last May, and this year they're putting in a thousand eleven-inch trout, but I reckon the water don't suit them.'

'Maybe they suit the pike,' said Gower as two boys dropped a large jack into a bin.

'It was a good trout stream when I was a boy,' said an old man, 'but they messed it up with dredging and the like.'

In the bin beside me a four-pound chub floated belly upwards. 'The bigger the fish the bigger the shock,' said Pritchard.

Later in the day, after we had returned to Long Wittenham, I recognized that same heavy-scaled form, still belly upwards, floating down-stream towards Clifton Hampden. With the rest of the morning's 'shock' he had been poured into the Thames. The several olive-skinned pike had slithered into the river as otters to their element; the roach lay on their silvery sides while gasping with surprise, the smaller chub looked upwards a trifle dazed. But the big white bellies with their orange fins needed a longer forget-fulness.

'He'll be right before he reaches Clifton bridge,' said Pritchard.

'He'll be back in these waters before dark,' said Gower.

On the following Saturday night, fifty-seven fisher-men ranging in age from eighteen to eighty-nine, and varying in size and weight as the contents of a creel, sat down to dinner at the Barley Mow by Clifton bridge. As fish less than eighteen inches in length are thrown back, so boys of less than eighteen years of age were thrown out if they appeared among the guests.

The achievements and the lack of achievements of the

past season's fishing and the prospects of the coming one were the main subjects of conversation. Last year's catches had been small in number, but the sizes of the individual fish had been large. No one could foretell what this year's might be. On one stretch of river the chub had moved up-stream, the pike from the Windrush would probably stay where they had been put in. The secretary remarked on how well Ken Bumpus had handled that ten-pounder pike last Sunday, with its jaws snapping in every direction. Even as it slid back into the water it had taken a small roach that was still numb from the electricity.

'Of course, pike are tough,' he said, 'the shock doesn't affect them as much as it does the other fish.'

'Tough as a crocodile,' said the president, who then told his story of a man he knew who had been savagely mauled by a crocodile after he had shot it dead. In my turn I mentioned the crocodile bird that goes into the open mouths of living crocodiles and picks their teeth for them, and I spoke of the small tropical fish I had seen go into the mouths of larger ones and in a similar way clean their teeth. Then we talked of salmon, and I confessed that once many years ago, on a dark night in Wales, I had stood beside a man with a torch while his brother with a gaff reaped from the river that ran through their farm a fish that they considered to be their due. 'After all, we breeds 'em up here,' he said to me.

'Why do salmon take a boiled shrimp, bright pink, when the like of them don't exist in fresh waters?' I was asked from across the table.

'Because,' I said, telling him the now established fact, 'the salmon when it goes to the sea feeds on deep-water shrimps and they are red, not green.'

After the loyal toast had been drunk, and those who had not already lit their cigarettes and pipes were told that they might smoke, a powerful fisherman took his place at the piano, and with arms that could land a sturgeon gave us a musical interlude. His hands hit chords on the keyboard with the precision of hammers, his legs worked like pistons. From 'Sons of the Sea' he took us without a break to 'I love Susie' and thence to 'Oh, Johnny.' From there we crossed the channel to Galway Bay where, as my eyes grew moist, he asked if our mothers came from Ireland. The climax was reached when a young tenor stood up and led the company in 'The Rose of Tralee.' Not a man that did not open his throat with emotion, not a throat that lacked a lubricant.

Then we had stories illustrated with playing cards, and stories that needed no added colour; and later the chief trophy of the club, the President's Cup, was passed round, filled and filled again with port. A magnificent cup, French eighteenth century, of glass mounted in finely chased silver and adorned with dolphins and a swan. Port is a wonderful linctus for the vocal chords, and in no time at all the second part of the concert had broken out. When shortly after closing time I slipped away from the assembly, the landlord was trying to make his sad refrain of 'Time, gentlemen, please,' heard above a barrage of 'Danny boys,' and down the road as I went my way

I could hear the pipes still calling—for just one more round.

Next morning I took up my *Observer* and read: 'Salmon are on the run. They have finished a period of tremendous gorging in the deep sea. Where no net could reach them, they have pastured for two, three, and four years over the lightless slopes that plunge down into the abyss. Their flesh is stained astaxanthin pink from the dye permeating the huge population of shrimps and little crustaceans that have provided the dark and continuous banquet. With nose and with smelling apparatus situated in their flanks the salmon have sought out their prey, and now, fat and strong, a new impulse overcomes them. They must mate.'

As Ned Topham had remarked to me at the dinner, 'There's a lot to be said for a good meal.'

CHAPTER TEN

THE FISHING by electricity had been in the valley of the Windrush, and in the course of searching for the appointed stretch of river we had passed through the village of Taynton. Stone! Walls of houses, walls of fields and gardens, glowing mellow and golden, they rose out of the ground as naturally and harmoniously as rocks outcropping from a hillside. Each stone seemed alive in its functioning: walls were like communities of purposeful entities, even as the polyps of a coral reef.

'Where did the stone come from?' I inquired of a man who was standing by a gate with a sheep-dog.

'Same place as St Paul's Cathedral,' he answered, 'out of yon hill to east.'

'Are the quarries still working?' I asked.

'Working again these past twenty years,' he said. 'They were closed down for a long time before that, near on a hundred years, they say. O' course, they be old operations, maybe a thousand years old.'

'Would it be possible for me to see them?' I asked.

'You go and ask Mr Lee,' he said. 'That's his farm. Turn left at foot of hill and drive through the gate. Never mind little dogs—they only bark.'

A few days later I returned to the village and drove through the gate, paying no attention to the little dogs who behaved as predicted. House and farm buildings, walls and roofs, all of the same sun-warmed stone; a long open shed, its roof supported in front by a row of stone pillars, sheltered carts and wagons. Mr Lee came from the house to greet me.

'Go through that far gate and follow the track across the hill—you can't miss it,' he said after I'd told him my purpose. 'You can't miss the quarry,' he repeated; 'you'll see the two cranes. Not working there to-day: too busy on the farm.'

But busy though he was he had time to lead me through the farm and set me on the path across the fields. And as we went he told me that the Romans had known and appreciated the Taynton stone—one of their coffins, six feet seven inches in length from a single block, had been found a short distance away. It was quite true, he said, that in the rebuilding of St Paul's after the Great Fire of 1666 much Taynton stone had been used—carried by road to the Thames at Eynsham and Radcot and floated down on barges to London.

'It was a Taynton man, Thomas Strong, whom Sir Christopher Wren appointed Master Mason. The

Strongs were a well-known family of Cotswold masons, and Thomas had inherited the quarries—they'd been owned by his family for generations. His father had been a great mason too—he'd worked under Nicolas Stone who was a colleague of Inigo Jones and Master Mason to Charles I. Thomas Strong had already worked under Wren at Oxford, and Wren had taken a liking to him. Of course, Strong was glad to find a good market for his stone, with the rebuilding of the City of London, and he'd acquired a site in the City near Paul's Wharf, for landing the stone from the barges.'

'How long did it take, the rebuilding of St Paul's?' I asked.

'Thirty-three years it took,' said Mr Lee. 'It was Thomas Strong who laid the foundation stone, and when they came to the end of it, it was his brother Edward, an old man then, who helped Sir Christopher's son to lay the last stone on the lantern above the dome.'

Three centuries earlier at Windsor they had used more than two thousand tons of stone from Taynton in the castle, and in the eighteenth century great quantities of it were purchased for the building of Blenheim Palace.

'It's the best weather-resisting stone in the country,' said Mr Lee. 'Look at Merton College in Oxford— part of it was built of Taynton stone in thirteen seventy something and you can still see the marks of the chisel. And Burford Church—the cathedral of the Cotswolds, they call it—built about 1150 and never a stone has had to be replaced. That fan vaulting in St George's

Chapel at Windsor was Taynton too,' he added; 'time of Henry VII—must be the finest ceiling in the world.'

With all this in my mind I expected to find huge amphitheatres cut out of the hillside, vast cavities similar to the chalk pits in the South Downs, though less amorphous in their cleavages. Instead I traversed a hillside whose ancient shallow scars were smoothed over with a coverlet of grass and herbs.

Later, in the dense woods that crest the hill behind the present workings, I came on the deeper dells of even earlier excavations, whence many an earth-bound sprite must have been set free when rocks were opened. Seldom have I wandered in such fay-peopled glades, where every freckled bole was smooth as human limb, where deep pits brimmed with beech and chestnut and in shallower goblets drifts of crimson willowherb glowed like wine.

Two cranes stood sentinel above the present crescentic quarry—a mere scratch on the hill, scarce half an acre of the surface tilth disturbed, twenty feet deep at most. And not more than half of it showed signs of being worked. Here was the source of the polished and carved interior panelling of the New Bodleian Library in Oxford.

The chain from one of the cranes was tight around the waist of a large cream-coloured slab of stone that rested on others of similar colour but variable shape, all of them leaning one on another against the side of the pit. A pickaxe lay beside one of them, three crowbars stood drunkenly amongst others, a broken barrow rested on its wheel and one leg in a heap of rubble.   It was as if life had ceased as suddenly as at Pompeii when the lava fell.   But there were no ashes here: cattle grazed peacefully, almost dangerously, on the verge of the pit, and across the Coombe Brook in the valley below crops were springing green.

On the pasture land beside the crane, 'benches' of stone were piled one on another, the semicircular marks of the drill catching the sunlight.   On an unhewn rock within the pit lay steel 'plugs and feathers' for splitting the stone into manageable sizes.   The principle is that of the double bevel, two wedges driven against each other in opposing directions so that the resultant outward pressure is exerted from all along their length and not at one particular point.   In cutting a stone, holes are drilled about six inches apart in a straight line, and into each of these a pair of 'feathers' is dropped.   Then between the upward tapering faces of the metal a steel wedge is driven downwards.   My sculptor friend Seamus Murphy, in his book *Stone Mad*, gives the feel and colour of the process when he writes: 'You'd often have to put in seven wedges in a row and then run along with a five-pound hammer tipping them, like a man playing a dulcimer, until you get them tight.'   To this a friend of his comments: 'The part I liked best was tapping with the heavy sledges as soon as the wedges were tight. 'Tis a mystery to me to this day how a few taps from a short-handled sledge could split a big stone, and a funny thing about it, you'd always get notice that it was going to break. I don't know how it is but you'd get the feeling that it's just on the verge of splitting when sure enough it would burst in two.'

Another of his fraternity of 'the Dust' tells how in the old days they made use of timber wedges, usually oak. 'They'd pour water on them when they were in and after a few days they'd swell and burst the stone. . . . But 'twouldn't do to-day. 'Twould be like waiting for the crops to grow if you were hungry.'

I have quoted from this book elsewhere and I'll be surprised if I don't do so again, for it is full of infectious enthusiasm for those with whom that artist learned his craft. He tells of the man who did his best to lead a good life but spent a lot of time thinking about sin; and of 'poor Johnny who had no interest in life but tombstones and graveyards . . . dead long before they closed his eyes, dead to everything in the world—but stone.' It is an affectionate and valuable record of men 'who with hammer, mallet, and chisel shaped and fashioned rough boulders.'

That was the wonder to me as I looked down on the rough boulders within the Taynton Quarry—that such seemingly intractable material could ever be mastered by a mallet and a chisel, could one day be transfigured.

Lower on the hillside stood a shed with a carbor-undum wheel for cutting the rough 'benches' of stone into rectangular slabs.   My fingers itched, for thus in days gone by had stone been delivered to me for carving.   The first piece that ever I touched with chisel came from the Portland quarries, a slab some four feet square and about six inches thick.   It was to be a low relief.   Several people have since called it a very low relief.   It began with a photograph that I saw in the souvenir programme of a Paris music-hall—two girls dancing, their arms interlocked to make a geometric pattern.   From that, with the substitution of a male figure for one of the dancers, a composition of more virile implication evolved on paper.

'Would it carve?' I asked Eric Gill when next he visited my studio.

'It jolly well should,' he said.

So a few days later when we met in London he took me to a toolsmith and chose for me chisels, claws, points, a pitching tool, and a couple of hammers, and on his next visit to my home showed me how they should be used.   It looked simple enough as I watched him.

Of the various technical difficulties that I encountered as time went on, the one which I remember most clearly was that every now and again the stone would 'pluck,' which meant that just as I was getting an approximation to the modelling of a limb a piece of stone the size of a split walnut would lift right out from my gradated surface.   You cannot replace such fragments—there is nothing to do but start again and reduce the whole level by the depth of the flaw.

When that level is scarcely higher than the depth of the flaw, it means that all surrounding surfaces are likewise implicated.

Pauses in any work are wonderful opportunities for the digestion of new ideas concerning it, and at that time, busy as I was with the Golden Cockerel Press and the artists and authors who worked for it, there were many enforced interludes during which, with sleeves unrolled and attending only to books, I got the feel of the stone better than if my biceps had been bulging. Eventually there came a day when I felt that to take away any more stone from my carving would not add to its significance, so with a prayer for the mellowing of time and weather I put it in my garden. To-day it stands on the lawn of the Hind's Head Hotel at Bray-on-Thames, whence visiting connoisseurs of art sometimes write me appreciative letters; others, less lit' ate, put their mark direct upon the stone.

Soon after that I acquired a retreat in London, a studio in Redcliffe Road. From an entrance hall decorated with plaster casts of figures in the classic style, modelled by a relative of the lady proprietor, there stretched a corridor with some thirty studios opening from it at regular intervals. There, in Number 14, I could work in peace, with any meals that I might need brought to me on a tray by Milly, daughter of the housekeeper and as lovely a girl as ever Renoir painted. The only interruptions to my thoughts were the succession of tappings at the studio door. 'Want a model?' was the inevitable greeting when I answered a summoning rap. There was unemployment at that time, and men and women of every age sought shillings for a few hours' work.

'Slep' in the waitin' room, Victoria, last night. Didn't 'ave no breakfast. Give us a few bob, gov'nor, and I'll sit for you 'ow you like.'

It was from one such girl that I did my next carving. She told me that she was training to be an acrobatic dancer, but had a stiffness in the hips that prevented her getting as low in 'the splits' as she would have liked.

'Get as low as you can on the floor,' I said, 'and I'll do a drawing.'

From several that I made, fore and aft, I carved a torso in Bath stone. Then there came to me a lady of title who said that she did not wish to be paid; she just felt that her figure would be of interest to an artist. It was, and from it I did a small relief, with water lapping at the thighs. Soon after that came Hugh Walpole wanting for his garden in Cumberland a figure in stone that could only have been carried out in bronze—limbs at the stretch, holding a spear, unmonumental. I compromised with a figure in stone—elemental, I hoped.

We have all heard of sculptors who see within their rough-hewn stone the figure that needs only to be set free by their hands. That day on Taynton hill, as I fingered the slabs still fresh from pit and wheel, with their quarry sap still soap-like to the touch, I sensed a timeless rhythm; sediment, millions of years dormant in darkness, a few centuries in fashioned form, and then again to chaos and to dust.

CHAPTER ELEVEN

WHEN IT became known in the village that I was interested in 'things natural,' people began to bring me oddments that they had picked up, for identification or explanation. Ian and Hugh, eleven-year-old twins from across the road, brought me two starlings' eggs, identical in every way, which they had found on their lawn. How did it happen, they asked, that the eggs could have been dropped together on the grass as closely as if they had been laid in a nest? I could only tell them that starlings are prone to lay an occasional egg in the open, and suggest that this particular bird might have had difficulty in laying the first egg and that during the delay the second one also had reached maturity.

Then came four little girls, about eight years old, with two eggs of larger size and differing in shape and colour, one being olive brown and pear-shaped, the other pale greenish grey and oval. They had found them, they said, in a deserted nest under brambles on the edge of a thicket, and there had been eleven of the brown ones and three of the grey. My answer to this problem was that the eggs of pheasants vary a great deal and that two birds often lay in the same nest.

A week later Mercy—of the Chinese geese—arrived with a brownish-yellow slug that had a fragment of shell attached to its hinder end. This, I could assure her, was normal, the scale being a rudiment of the full shell of snails, near relations to the slugs. But what I didn't know until I looked into a history of the British Mollusca was that this particular species, *Testacella haliotidea*, is carnivorous and innocent of any harm to young greens. Its main diet is earthworms, and it is able to elongate its body so that it can follow and seize the worms in their burrows.

The earthworms by their workings keep our soil fertile, yet gardeners pour poison on lawns to kill the creatures by the million; the carnivorous slugs kill the earthworms, yet gardeners destroy all slugs at every opportunity. What hope is there of international peace?

Following on the heels of the slug came the empty carcasses of seven bumble-bees. They had been found close together under a guelder rose-bush, and each had been so completely eviscerated that the interiors of their body cavities shone as though polished, shone as the pollen-bearing segments of their hinder legs. I sent the sad husks to the Institute of Entomology and in due course the reply came back: 'Four species of bumble-bee, all females, represented in the collection.

Probably caught by some small animal such as a shrew when they were emerging from hibernation and still lethargic. The high polish may have been effected by ants.'

Polish though not quite so bright was also on a coin brought to me by Arthur, who is as skilful in a garden as he is at a carpenter's bench. He had dug it up when preparing a seed bed in his allotment, and it proved to be a Jetton or token made in the sixteenth century by Hans Krauwinchel of Nurenburg. Several of these have been found in the neighbourhood.

Then came an elder of the village with a phial of 'Brine Shrimp Eggs' which, for some reason, he wanted me to hatch. 'Sprinkle on fresh water to which common salt has been added,' read the directions. Not only did I obey the instructions but I persuaded a friend then visiting the Scilly Isles to bring me back her sponge-bag filled with seaweed. My large glass container became a picture of romance, a submarine photographer's dream: brown delicately fingered weed spiralled upwards from variegated pebbles; green weed dainty as a young lettuce grew from a fan shell; a small sea-urchin, exposing its profusion of tubular feet, moved slowly from side to side across the inner surface of the glass.

'Eggs will hatch in 24–48 hours,' said the instructions. They were still floating at 96 hours. At 164 hours I noticed a purple tint spreading upwards from my sea floor, translucent, fluorescent as it came towards the surface. At 216 hours I put my nose to the open mouth of the jar.

Have you ever heard of the Bruce Quick Return Method of Compost-Making for the garden? You pile lawn mowings, tea leaves, cabbage leaves, coffee grounds, clearings from the flower-beds and debris from the kitchen, and keeping them well covered add from time to time as you go a few drops of 'herbal activator.' Within weeks you have a succulent black compost which brings richer colours to the flower-beds and brighter roses to the cheeks of those who spread it on their vegetable beds. You have even the means of growing cabbages that do not smell when cooking. I added the seaweed to my compost bin and poured the purple liquid on to the asparagus bed. Pray God that ere this book is published a few of those tender shoots may have yielded thanks for this salinity.

Other strains and stresses were also occurring just then. During the last few days of March two male blackbirds in my garden fought to the death, he of the brighter yellow bill being the victor. I only saw the fight when the conqueror was pecking furiously at the helpless body on the ground, and it was too late to intervene. His hen was aggressive also, swooping at any thrush that found a worm and carrying away the booty. A few days after the battle nest-building began within three yards of the scene, and in due course the first egg was laid. Next day there was a second egg, but on the third day instead of finding yet another in the nest I saw that one of the two already laid had disappeared. The hen laid no more but brooded the single egg until after fourteen days the chick, naked and pink as a new-born mouse, broke through its shell. Its life, however, was short, for by noon on the fifth day after hatching some predatory creature had taken it and the nest was empty.

Within forty-eight hours the parent hen had begun to build again, the new nest being in a different hedge and better concealed, nor did she go to and from it as directly as she had done in her first essay.   This time she entered the hedge some six feet from the nest and made her way to it through thick cover.   The foliage made it difficult for me to follow the course of her laying, but in due time four fledglings showed their yellow gapes above the edge of the nest and later fluttered on to the lawn.

Here by this gentle backwater I find a world where neighbourliness is the currency.   A farmer sees a patch of my garden looking starved and says: 'I'll send you along a load of manure in the morning.'   Mercy brings me double yolkers.   'Well, you're outsize—you need them,' she says.   I admire the cinerarias in a greenhouse across the road, and next day two of the brightest are at my door.   Best of all, a medical man drops in and says: 'You like the sun—there's a sandpit at the end of my garden just beside the river: it's private as a bath-room—you use it.'   I tell him that the sun gives me energy.   'Best tonic in the world,' he says.   And so I stretch my length as the Almighty made it, with the slight accretion that time has added, and when I rise I am a stronger man.

'Never read a book in my life,' another neighbour told me; 'don't reckon I need 'em.   Can sign cheques but the wife writes 'em.   Had fourteen pounds when I come here first, that was all.   Look at the place now!'

We were leaning over one of his farm gates, admiring a big Berkshire sow that was shortly due to pig.

'Soon after I come here,' he continued, 'I wanted to get married, so I goes along to the vicar.   "Vicar," I says, "I wants to get married but I got no money."

'"Have you got a girl?" says Vicar.

'"I got a girl," I said, "and she's a girl and a half."

'"All right," says Vicar.   "I'll marry you for nothing and you can pay me when you're rich."

'So he marries us, and what does my old cousin Tom from Taynton do but bring me two pounds as a wedding present.   So next day I goes along to Vicar.   "Vicar," I says, "I've got two pounds.   How much of that would you like for marrying us?"

'"No," he says, "you keep that.   You keep that for luck," he says.   And didn't it bring us luck! Five lovely children, and look at the farm now.   Fifty-seven head of cattle, seventeen cows in milk.'

'How many did you have when you came here?' I asked.

'Didn't have any—not a one!   Bought the first with the fourteen pound.   Had trouble to get her, too. Market, market, every week and not a one for the price.   Then I came on a Jersey with calf for sixteen pound, so I bought the two and sold the calf for two pound.   That left only the fourteen to pay.'

As I was leaving him I asked if he could do with a few barrow loads of coarse gravel that had been left over from my path.

'Just right for *my* path,' he said. 'I'll send the boy along for it.'

Next evening I joined him again as he was watching his pig.

'You know that lock on your back gate?' he said. 'You left it open for the boy. The boy says it's no good, says he could open it with two taps of a stone. I said to him, didn't you tell the man—he didn't put it there for nothing.'

'I haven't seen him since,' I said.

'I'll send him over to-night, 'bout six o'clock—would you be in? He'll fix it for you. No good having a lock like that.'

'Nothing like pigs for significant form, Bob,' interrupted a small man who had banged the door of an ancient car and come from the road to join us. Though I did not recognize him at first, there was something familiar about the untidy twist of his necktie and the eager eyes that looked out from under two unkempt shocks of hair. 'Haven't seen you in twenty years,' he said to me. 'Only heard last week that you were hereabouts.'

'Near fifty years since the Slade,' I said at a guess.

'More than forty anyway,' he said.

I knew who he was then—Giotto Junior, as we used to call him because of his obsession with the early Florentine artists and because of the intensity of his own religious paintings.

'Pigs, I could draw them all day long,' he said, 'but they're awkward in a studio.'

Though I had followed his work through the years, I

had never known him put pencil to pig.   Saints and angels and humans in mystic communion: allegories, they were his line, at times difficult to comprehend but always combining a richness of form with minute and loving detail.

He was worrying about an article which some publisher had commissioned from him, when he heard that I had come to the district: an autobiography or a philosophy of his work—he didn't quite know what they wanted and hoped I might be able to help him.   But then, fumbling in his pockets, he found he had forgotten to bring the letters about it.   Never mind, it was Tuesday and he'd be passing again on Thursday—some function in his honour in Oxford that he had to attend.

As he walked ahead of me towards the cottage I noticed that his shiny blue serge trousers had a slit across their seat, and through it was hanging a wide flap of linen shirt immaculately white.   I said nothing, but when two days later he paid his return visit I saw that the rent had been mended by a rectangular patch of mustard red tweed which spread from side to side of his behind.

'Why, Giotto,' I said, 'what's happened to you? You're all poshed up.'

'Oh yes, I know,' he said wearily.   'But I'm going to a reception.'

Giotto was the master draughtsman among the students of our generation at the Slade.   Form and its interpretation obsessed him: I remember when a huge South African joined us in the life room, Giotto who was short of stature stood looking up at his face.

'May I stroke your nose?' he asked at length, and having run his finger along the high crest of that feature returned to his easel and drew it.

Life drawing was the beginning and but a step removed from the end of all study at the Slade in those days. Colour didn't matter; it was something laid on afterwards, almost as a house decorator works. To see men scrubbing colours together on their palette until they found a flat dull tone of mud used to distress me, for I had worked under a man who couldn't draw a finite line to any form but could make his pigments sparkle almost as the French Impressionists had done. Clean, cold, unrelenting drawing with a hard pencil was the order: no 'sketching,' none of the charcoal don't-give-yourself-away school: and Giotto, though physically the smallest student in the class, was with pencil in his hand the biggest man among us.

CHAPTER TWELVE

IT IS ONLY a few years since there lived in the
village a beautiful young girl of some seventeen
summers. Her parents' house was close to the
river, and often Dawn—for that was her name—
would wander by the water noticing the many forms of

reeds and rushes that grow there, the sedges with their varied foxtail plumes, the branching bur-reed with its globular clusters of white flowers and spiky seed pods, the sweet sedge with horn-like flower cones springing from its bladed leaf. Sometimes she would gather bunches of these and bring them home to spread on the stone floor of the hall for the sweet scent that came from them when crushed. The flowers, too, she greeted in their seasons, marigolds and celandines, comfrey, loosestrife, and willowherb, in particular the 'flowering rush'—which is not a rush at all—whose rose pink petals follow so closely on those of the white and golden water lilies.

One day in late spring she found a wild duckling, 'no bigger than would fit in a coffee cup,' lying helpless and deserted. Dawn picked it up, dried it as best she could with her handkerchief, and opening her blouse put it close against her bosom. She took it home and fed it on bread and milk and worms, keeping it always, both day and night, next her skin for warmth. The little creature throve and soon, fully feathered, became one of the family, with its own box of straw in their drawing-room.

Dawn and the duck came to tea in my garden, each as composed as the other. Dawn ate fruit cake from a plate, the duck took meal-worms from my hand. One thing that hurt me a little at first was that when a fourth member of our party, another girl, held out further meal-worms, the duck uttered the sweetest of chortlings to her as it accepted the offering.

'You see,' said Dawn, 'it's a drake—not very

noticeable just now in eclipse—and he knows the difference.'

'Between man and woman?' I asked in surprise.

Dawn nodded. 'He displays to me and Mother, never to Dad,' she said. 'Sometimes he'll come along giving a sort of quick lift to his head with the feathers all puffed out, and then he'll try to get hold of the skin on the backs of our hands and hold it like a drake does to the neck of a duck in the water. He never does that to Dad or another man.'

Here are we, *Homines sapientes*, I thought, unable to distinguish between the male and female of many birds, and yet a two-year-old drake can tell at a glance a male from a female of the human species, even though both are wearing slacks.

This behaviour on the part of the drake would seem to contradict the statement of Konrad Lorenz, 'the modern Fabre,' that in birds 'there is no law of attraction of opposites, by which female animals are drawn towards men and males towards women.' Nevertheless what I have said is factual.

Lorenz, in his book *King Solomon's Ring* from which I have quoted, has many tales to tell from his own experiences with birds who, deprived of their normal parents or associations, have automatically transferred their instinctive reactions to those human beings with whom they have been in contact. In some cases the circumstances were accidental, in others they were brought about by deliberate experiment, as when the author quacked to a brood of young mallard while they were emerging from their shells in an incubator.

Whereas others of the same species for whom he did not imitate the mother notes had on being taken from the incubator run from him and hidden in a dark corner, these lifted their gaze confidently, scuttled after him, and thenceforth treated him as a parent.

He tells also of a peacock in the Vienna Zoo that, during a period of extreme cold, was put into the reptile house for warmth, and ever after directed its desire and its display towards giant tortoises.

From the Zoo at Amsterdam comes another example of this deviation. There, A. F. J. Portielje reared a male South American bittern which when mature made advances to human beings. Not only that but after a female of the species had been found for him he refused for a long time to pay her any attention. When eventually he did take interest and the birds began to breed, it was only necessary for Portielje to go near their nest for the male bird to rush at the female and, driving her away, invite this foster-parent with much ceremony to take her place on the nest.

Among other caprices of instinct Jane, a fox terrier resident in the village of Kingham, in the valley of the Evenlode, has recently been showing originality. When it happened that she and a cat in her household were about to have families at the same time, and the kittens began to arrive a few hours ahead of the puppies, Jane nipped across to the cat's box and stole kitten after kitten as it was born, eventually leaving but one of the litter to its rightful mother. Then when her own offspring arrived she brought up both families as one. This might have been hard on the cat had not

compensation been at hand.   A neighbour knowing of
the terrier's maternal capabilities, but not having heard
of the transfer of kittens, brought to the house two
puppies that needed fostering.   These received the
warmest of welcomes from the cat, who thereupon
cherished them as her own and reared them with the
one kitten that had been left to her.

Jane's instinctive reactions are strong.   When one
of her offspring gave birth to a litter, she produced
milk and helped to rear it, even though she herself had
had no family for two years.

CHAPTER THIRTEEN

EARLY IN APRIL a second robin appeared in my garden, and I hoped that the pair might build where I could watch them. Far from it. Just at the time when I should have seen the hen gathering leaves and moss for their nest, the two birds vanished, and for weeks I saw nothing of either of them.

'Seen anything of a pair of robins?' I called over the hedge to my neighbour, Dick Gower.

'Dammit,' he said, 'I haven't been able to dig in the garden for the past week—they're nesting in the handle of my spade. It was leaning up against the wall in the shed and the hole in the handle just suited them and there they are. First egg this morning.'

Some two weeks later the cock, after fluttering across the window of my studio, presented himself at the door. I went outside, for where papers and drawings are lying about birds are not always the most considerate guests, and I threw him a meal-worm. He took it, gave it a couple of quick flicks as if to numb it, and swallowed it. The second worm that I threw he flicked in a similar way but did not swallow, holding it across his beak instead, as if waiting for more. Three more he took and held in the same way, then when I had given him a fifth and his beak resembled some Medusa-like miniature of writhing serpents, he took wing and dipped over the boundary hedge.

I was hardly settled again at my easel before that bird

had returned, expectant. This time he did not swallow even one worm: he fitted four of them across his beak and departed.   Again and again that morning and many times in the evening he came back; I reckoned that he must have carried away some seventy or more worms in the day.   The same happened next day and the day following, and for more than a week after with ever increasing demands.   Then one morning he seemed coy, hovering awhile in the neighbourhood before coming to his accustomed perch in the young plum-tree.   Then he ate two worms and only troubled to carry one away.   I did not see him again until next morning, by which time another change in the cycle had set in: the stimulus to feed others had relaxed and without that urge his own appetite had returned.   In less than an hour he consumed twenty-two worms. Before the day was out he had swallowed a further twenty-three.

Of the maximum number of nine that he could consume at a sitting, the first seven were taken as rapidly as I could throw them one at a time, then would come a moment's contemplation before the eighth.   Between that and the limit of his internal capacity there was a longer pause, and more than once I thought I noticed a movement in the throat that might have been a nice quiet belch.

As time went on the bird became more and more tame, sitting on the lid of the teapot when I had morning tea in the garden, ready at any moment to perch on my hand and take a meal-worm.   When his second family had hatched and begun to make their

demands, he cast off all caution and came through the
open door of my studio with as little self-consciousness
as on that first afternoon when he played film star on
the newly laid cement floor. Dr Roget's *Thesaurus*
which lay on my writing-table became his favourite
perch, and there on its firm binding he would flick
and tap his beakful of worms into their correct align-
ment before flying with them over the fence to his new
nest. Soon his presence became so constant and his
demands so persistent that in order to concentrate on
my work I had to keep the door and all windows shut.
And the weather had turned hot. There came an
afternoon when the temperature reached eighty and,
reminded of Samoa, I thought of my lava-lava. It
didn't take long to get rid of shirt and trousers and to
gird my loins in the blue-and-white flowered strip of
cotton. And just then the churchwarden and his wife
arrived to pay me their first social call.

But in due course the young robins were fledged and

able to fly. They came into my garden and there all
four of them would hop around my feet ready at any
moment to pick up a worm that I might throw them or
to crouch with yellow-edged gape wide open for what
their parent would shove down their throats.   How
long, I wondered, before instincts would change and
they would be as ruthlessly driven from the territory
as just then they were being assiduously cared for?

It was the day when the four youngsters had followed
their parent on to my garden table that a lady said to
me: 'How can you spend so much time and energy on a
robin?'

I answered in effect: 'How can you spend so much
time and energy on that dog of yours that even when
sitting at your side must be kept on a lead lest he
murder the cat?   He has to be taken out for exercise
every day of the year,' I said; 'he can't be left alone for
more than a day and he can't even sing.   My robin
causes me no responsibility; his housing arrangements
are his own affair.   If I leave him for days on end he
does not suffer, and almost throughout the year I can
hear his song.'

As the lady was being argumentative I did not add
that, in spite of what I'd said, the best companions
of my youth had been dogs, and that the only reason I
didn't keep a couple now was that I couldn't spare the
time to which they were entitled.

It wasn't long indeed before instincts did change in
those birds.   Only on that one day did all five of them
sit together on my table, with no jealousies in their
hearts.   From then on they became more and more

quarrelsome until at the end of a fortnight there was rarely more than one present at a time.

When first the young ones came to the table, they made no attempt to pick up the worms that I threw to them, waiting for their parent to push three or four at a time into their open gapes. But gradually they began to show initiative, though only when the father was not present. The moment that he put in an appearance they relapsed into helplessness and dependence, crouching beside a worm with open mouths as if incapable of picking it up. Then after another few days they began to rival him in agility, snapping up any grub that came near them before he could get to it, even though if he did get to it first he invariably gave it to one of them. It was curious to watch the growing look of surprise and almost of reproach on the old bird's face as the young ones became increasingly independent. I began to see less and less of him and wondered if he had not solaced himself by starting yet another family. I began too to see less of the family, their number decreasing like the Nigger Boys, from

Four little robins sitting on my table
Gobbling up meal-worms as fast as they are able,

to

One little robin with tummy pretty tight
Glaring all around him, ready for a fight.

I was sorry when that petulant youngster gained the ascendancy, for his nature had by no means the charm of others in the family. One in particular had from its earliest days been brighter of eye and more confiding, and I had hoped that if dominion had to pass it might be in its direction.   But no—perhaps that charmer was a female and my unconscious susceptibilities akin to those of Dawn's duck—the lot fell upon a most ungentle bully; not only ungentle but morose, for when as time went on the undefeated members of the family, including the father, hovered near not daring to approach his throne, my table, and I threw them worms, now right, now left, he would pay no attention to the worms that I had offered him but would sit there glowering, heavy-eyed and sulky, no model for a Christmas card at all.

Days went by and weeks passed with that bird in sole command.   Then came a surprise: another robin, a stranger and a much younger one, appeared on my lawn.   Whereas the bully and its generation were daily adding red to their breasts, this little one was still in speckled adolescence.   It came to my garden alone, no sign of parents or kindred, and on its first visit seemed content to busy itself on the lawn and in the rose-beds.   But next morning it was waiting for me on my table, and the former occupier had disappeared.   Once only in the days that followed did the older bird come back and then but for a momentary visit.   The much younger newcomer had quietly and without any fuss usurped the position, and strangely enough it was far tamer and more gentle than any of the others had been.   No trace of fear or shyness: it perched on the seat close beside me, it ate from my hand, and when I brought out my breakfast tray it perched on the butter-dish and helped itself.

'You want to mind them robins,' said a farmer's wife in the village when I went to buy bran for my meal-worms. 'Last year one of them came through the door into this house and next day my husband had an accident and broke his leg.'

CHAPTER FOURTEEN

IN THE BUS to Wallingford one April day, I found myself sharing a seat with seventy-year-old Daniel from my own parish. He didn't say much for the first mile of the road, indeed his only sign of activity, physical or mental, was when a cock pheasant crossed the road ahead of us. Then his shoulders stiffened and his hands twitched.

It wasn't until we were going through Little Wittenham that, jerking a thumb towards the one remaining wall of a cottage, he turned to me.

'Lived there for years,' he said. 'Lived there till I got married—that's forty years ago. Place was fallin' down then; anyway she didn't like me going out so much o' nights, so we moved to Long Wittenham and there I been ever since.'

'What took you out at night?' I asked, for even to-day in Little Wittenham there isn't a pub where you can sit down.

'Poaching,' he said, lowering his voice. 'Every Saturday regular and many another night as well I'd be out, and the number of rabbits I had you wouldn't

believe.   And the fun I had, too—makes me laugh
now to think of it.   I remember one night,' he said,
'when I was coming home with five of them—I had one
down each leg of me trousers, with their hind legs
hitched round me braces, one tied round me waist
inside me shirt, and one in each of me big inside
pockets—and I met the policeman.   A nice honour-
able man he was, fair to all.

'"I suppose," he says, "you'll be working late
to-night."'

'"No," I says, "I'm on me way home."'

'"Aren't you havin' any sport these times?" he
says.

'"No," I says; "given it all up a long while back."'

'"Ah well," he says, "if you should be taking a
short cut across the fields on your way home and you
get tripped up by a rabbit, drop it in over my gate as
you go by."'

'"Don't worry," I says, "I've got one on me now."'

'Down in Wittenham Wood I used to go regular,'
continued Daniel.   'There was plenty of rabbits there
then and a nice few birds too.   But the best bit of
sport ever I had was one day when I was trimming
timber in that wood—they kept it very orderly in
those days—and one way or another I lost me billhook.
So I goes along to ask the loan of one from a fellow livin'
in a caravan by the side of the wood—a professional
trapper he was, employed by the squire; and when I
get to the caravan he's asleep inside, and outside on the
ground is a pile of rabbits.   Threescore or more there
must have been, all heaped up and gutted.   A pity to

wake him, I thought, so I took a couple of the rabbits, put 'em in me pocket and went off to where I knew was a patch of stinging-nettles, and I dropped 'em in there. And then I was wanting that billhook and I began to wonder was he awake yet. So I goes back to the caravan again and the fellow was snoring. It's a pity not to have a few more of them rabbits, I thought, so I took another couple and carried 'em off to the stinging-nettles. Would you believe it, when I went back half an hour later the man was still snoring, so this time I took four—I couldn't bear to leave 'em behind. And next day I met him in Brightwell and he hadn't noticed them lost. ''Come and have a drink, Dan,'' he says, and he stood me a pint.'

'And the billhook?' I asked.

'Stuck in the fork of a birch-tree,' said Daniel. 'Someone must 'a' found it and put it there for me. Folks are very honest in these parts.'

CHAPTER FIFTEEN

WHEN YOU are deep in contemplation of other things there isn't much difference in the back of your mind between a Saracen and a Philistine. I had spent two mornings engraving the miniature Crusader who lies in St Mary's church, two lovely late April mornings when pent-up leaves were pouring from every sprig and fruit buds were swelling, impatient to explode. Somehow there came forward into my consciousness the story of Samson and Delilah, and I remembered a painting long since begun but never finished. With other canvases it stood with its face against the studio wall.

No Samson in the village, little chance of a Delilah, but up came the canvas to the easel. I'll work from memory and imagination, I thought. If imagination is concentrated race experience there should be no drought of ideas. Hasn't the subjugation of the male by the female, by one means or another, been an age-long industry?

The moment in the narrative that I had chosen to illustrate was when Delilah having enticed Samson, as the Lords of the Philistines had commanded her, was 'vexing his soul unto death' so that he was about to tell her the secret of his strength—his unshorn locks and beard. From an artist's point of view the subject offers a wonderful concentration of elemental forms, but in terms of words it is delicate to pursue.

I had already worked out the design in an engraving which I did many years ago; now the immediate problem was colour. It has often seemed to me strange that goddesses, nymphs of the brake, and other classical heroines should be portrayed as if they had for the first time discarded their clothes. Surely their open-air life should have put a glint of gold into their skin? In the sixteenth-century painting by the Florentine Bronzino, 'Venus and Cupid,' now in the National Gallery in London, the naked lady is pale as the inside of a lemon rind. Born of the sea and not averse to daylight junketings, it is hard to believe that she would not have acquired at least the outer gloss of a pippin. But Delilah had been an indoor lass so this problem did not arise: I could make her pink as a show girl or pale as the dove-grey sands. With Samson there was little difficulty either. Swarthy from the sun, all I needed for him was sienna, raw and burnt—adjectives appropriate enough to the poor fellow himself.

Here I must tell of a friend of mine who, much to his wife's disapproval, grew a beard—not a dark one like Samson's but a fine blond growth with just a touch of auburn in it. There came a time when she disapproved of other things that he did, there came a time when she disapproved of everything that he did, so much so that there came a time when he went abroad, not quite sure if and when he would return. But as time passed she wrote and suggested that life together in a new country would put everything right and he, welcoming the idea, shaved off his beard so that his welcome to her might be the more complete.

'Yes,' she said to him that first evening as together they inhaled the evening scents of the tropics, 'everything here is marvellous. But for God's sake, do grow your beard again.'

My canvas progressed, though there were inevitable interruptions to my thoughts. One of the intervals was on the first really hot day of summer, the first Sunday in May, when I looked up and saw my pear-tree in its fullest bloom in bright sunshine. In the words of one of my correspondents, an Irish poetess: 'It put a pain in the pit of me guts.' The white flecks of cloud behind the tree were grey as old thatch, the blue sky above it was deep as thundercloud, the welter of its blossom blasted all things white to nondescript. During the winter the bare branches of the tree had reminded me again and again of the studied rhythms of ballet dancers, so apposite were they in their opposition; now the limbs were concealed under a froth of sequined furbelows. Now, too, swallows and swifts were circling high in the heavens, and at intervals from early till late the cuckoo was 'blowing.'

That evening I was dining with a neighbour, a lawyer, and as we drank our coffee he pointed to a black tin deed box under a table in a corner of the room. 'You'd be surprised at the records of cuckoos in the nest that that holds,' he said.

'Didn't know you dealt in divorces,' I answered.

'No divorces there—just adoptions,' he replied.

He got up and pulled the box from under the table.

'Come and have a look,' he said. 'I have records here of more than a hundred and fifty cases.'

As he lifted the lid I expected to see bundles of dreary documents tied up in tapes and spattered with sealing-wax.   Instead there opened before me an array of small glass-topped boxes, each of which held four or five eggs of wild birds.   I recognized robins, wagtails, bullfinches, pipits, and many of the warblers.

'That's only a few of them,' he said; 'there are five more layers under those, and in every box there's a cuckoo's egg.'

'But how did you come by them?' I asked.

'I know no more of their history,' he said, 'than the foster bird knows of the surprise packet in her nest. I came into this house five years ago, and I was here a year before I noticed the box lying in the cellar.   No one can tell me anything about it.'

Together we began to unpack the treasure chest and spread the contents on the floor.   As I expected, the eggs of pipits were greatly in the majority.   Of the hundred and sixty-five sets, representing thirty species of foster-parent, those of the meadow and tree-pipits, combined, made up a third, and in almost every case the cuckoo's egg was a near or perfect match for the mottled brown shells of the pipit.

Next in favour as a host was the pied wagtail, with sixteen clutches.   Here the matching of the intruder's egg, pale grey and finely stippled, was even more remarkable.   Then came fourteen examples from the reed warblers: brown eggs, more heavily blotched and marbled than the pipits' but as closely approximating. Four from nightingales' nests, though faintly freckled, partook of the deep olive-green of their fosterers.

But it was among the dunnocks, 'hedge-sparrows,' that the interest reached a climax. In four of the five clutches the intruder's egg showed no resemblance whatever to those of its host; but in the fifth it was blue—as blue as those beside it, with just a few small black spots as on a thrush's egg. I knew that but one or two, at the most, blue eggs from cuckoos had hitherto been recorded in England. Here apparently was a third.

From this to the tiny ochre or maroon-speckled eggs of willow-warbler, chiff-chaff, and wren was a sad come-down. In each case the cuckoo had laid an outsize muddy grey and dirtily mottled egg which bore no resemblance to the fragile porcelains by its side. Perhaps those few, four in all, were but emergency layings, like babies born in buses. After all, a bird is 'only human.'

'Now,' said my host, 'can you tell the court'—for by this time others had joined in the scrutiny—'can you tell the court by what means a cuckoo is able to lay eggs of so many different colours and seemingly each colour at will?'

'I think,' I said to him, ''tis the other way about and the bird finds a nest with eggs that match the only colour it can lay. Some domestic hens always lay brown eggs, some always lay white, and similar though more varied limitations apply to cuckoos. Each particular cuckoo always lays in a nest of the same species.'

Since my return to the countryside I had been glancing again at some of the bird books on my shelves, in particular *The Truth about the Cuckoo*, by Edgar Chance, and *Cuckoo Problems*, by E. C. Stuart Baker; the former an intensive study of the European cuckoo's behaviour in a small area of England, the other the result of seventy years' research into the habits of more than forty species of the bird in widely separated countries of the world. A few of the conclusions which I think would be accepted by both are that cuckoos search for the nests in which it will suit them to lay some days or at any rate hours before their time of laying; that they lay at intervals of approximately forty-eight hours, and that when placing an egg in a nest they remove one of the eggs of the foster-parent. They also agree that when the nest is one into which the cuckoo cannot enter, the egg is projected or 'squirted' instead of being laid in the usual manner. As to the morals of the birds, Mr Chance writes that he is 'encouraged to believe that cuckoos pair as faithfully as other birds': on the other hand, Mr Baker thinks that the female is promiscuous. But then Mr Baker had for the most part studied species whose habitat lies 'east of Suez,' and I am reminded of the late Lord Grey's remark on the common pheasants, polygamous by nature, that 'the inferiority of their habits is not native to Britain, and our country is not responsible.' In the same paragraph he stated that with few exceptions British birds are monogamous, giving the names of the offenders as the cuckoo, ruffs and reeves, black game, and capercailzie, several of which are not really indigenous to this country; but he forgot or did not know that the pied and the spotted flycatchers, the corn and the yellow buntings, the wren, the white-throat, and the marsh harrier are all known to depart from the matrimonial standards of an English gentle-man, and many others, including the bittern, are strongly suspect. Why, in Cornwall an observer noted that two corn buntings had each seven wives, and another that fifteen males of that species were mated with fifty-one females.

Next morning after a few soliloquies at dawn I put from my mind such distressing facts and turned my thoughts to the pure delights of painting.

CHAPTER SIXTEEN

ID MAY, orgastic May that makes riot in our gardens. Exultant choruses of colour were rushing across the lawns from bed to border, from border to bed. There was scarce time to sense their glee.

Among the petals of a yellow wallflower I noticed what seemed to be a cluster of tiny glass beads, yellow and black. A touch to the plant with my finger caused no stir among them, but a gentle breath sent them scurrying by invisible threads from bud to leaf tip, from petal to nearby tendril. The young of the garden spider, *Araneus diadematus*, so called because of the white jewel-like markings on its back. Fabre knew it as *Epeira diadema* and speaks of the nimble little acrobats being thrown into a state of tumult and confusion by the slightest breeze, for it is by the gossamer threads of their own spinning, carried on light airs, that the youngsters escape from the cannibalistic family circle and begin their solitary careers.

'Come and see my young spiders,' I called to a beautiful lady to whom I had been introduced the evening before and who happened to pass my gate.

'Anything but spiders—I can't bear them,' she answered.

'But they told me you're Oxford and Maths,' I said.

'What's that got to do with spiders?' she asked.

'Garden spiders weave their webs in logarithmic

spirals,' I told her, having just learned that fact from Fabre.

So she came into my parlour, and the first thing she did after glancing at the spiderlings was to pick up from beside my doorstep an ammonite, a fossil that with many others of the kind I had found a few days earlier on a chalk hill overlooking the Thame, a tributary of the Thames.

'Here also you have the logarithmic spiral,' she said, tracing with her finger the serrated whorls.

'Always thought of it as the horn of Ammon,' I said.

'Ammon?' she queried.

'Yes,' I said, 'the Egyptian god with a ram's head and curved horns.'

'But don't you see,' she said, and she began to talk in mathematical terms that were far beyond my comprehension.

'Let's consult the *Ox. Comp. to Literature*,' I said, leading her indoors. There, under *Ammonian Horn*, we read 'See Amalthea,' and under that heading we learned that Amalthea was a nymph who nursed the infant Zeus. She fed him with the milk of a goat, and it was the horn of this goat that became the symbol of , abundance—cornucopia, the horn of plenty.

'My name is Althea,' she said. 'I never knew I was classical.'

'Divine, according to the poet Lovelace,' I told her.

'"There is a divinity in *odd* numbers," according to Falstaff,' she answered; 'but,' with a sigh, 'all my dates are even: 22nd February 1928 I was born.'

'The *perfect* numbers are all even,' I said to comfort

her, 'and 28 is one of them.   And incidentally,' I
added, 'this year '56 is twice 28, the year of your birth
and your present age.'

I was talking about one of the few pretty patterns in
mathematics that I remember: only four 'perfect
numbers' under a million, that title being accorded to
those in which all the lesser numbers which divide it
evenly will when added together make up its sum.
The simplest is six: one goes into it six times, two goes
into it three times, three goes into it twice: and one,
two, and three added together make six.   The next in
the scale is 28.   One and two go into it, three doesn't,
four does, five and six don't, seven does: after that only
fourteen succeeds.   Add together one, two, four,
seven, and fourteen and behold, a total of 28.   Nothing
more of the kind till we get to 496, and nothing more
then till 8,128.   The next is 33,550,336, which
caused a philosopher who had sought diligently to
affirm that 'the good and the beautiful are rare and
easily counted, whereas the ugly and bad are prolific,'
a remark with which I do not agree.   A theologian
has said that the world was created in six days because
six is the first perfect number; and recently a prophet
from California has sought to prove the divine origin of
the Bible by the number seven and its multiples, which
occur 'in a mysterious and peculiar manner beneath the
very surface' of the Hebrew and Greek texts.   He
doesn't say from which one of the many Greek texts he
made his calculation.

CHAPTER SEVENTEEN

LOOKING from my garden I can see the Wittenham Clumps cresting the twin slopes of Sinodun
Hill—known to poets as the Maiden's Breasts,
to those of other temperament as Mother
Dunch's Buttocks.   And from under the silken beeches
that canopy those crests I can see the Thames looping
its way south and east from Abingdon.   There the
Ock, born of those hills from which the great White
Horse of Wessex has for two thousand years shone
across the vale, brings in its waters.   Quietly it has
puddled its way through the history-laden arable and
pasture lands, with hardly a field beside its banks that
has not yielded relics of ancient times: lead coffins,
bronze weapons and utensils, fragments of pottery, and
coins innumerable, many of them dating from the reign
of Constantine the Great.   He it was whose troops at

York in A.D. 306 proclaimed him Caesar.   He it was
who when marching against his rival Maxentius in Rome
saw in the sky a great luminous cross with the words
In hoc signo vince and became a convert to Christianity,
and he it was who transferred the capital of the Roman
Empire to Byzantium and named it Constantinople.

The swelling of the hillock hides from me the
junction of the Thame with the greater river whose
name henceforth is undisputed.   Isis on marriage has
yielded up her identity.   Like the Ock, weirs and
disused corn mills punctuate the course of this new
tributary as, many times dividing and combining again,
it flows from beyond Aylesbury some thirty miles
north-east, whence come our swan-white ducks.   The
white horse, mightiest of its hill-cut breed in England,
gallops across the hill above the springing waters of the
Ock; the huge white ducks dibble in the brooklets of
the Thame.   No lack of history, either, on the Thame,
from earthworks near its source to Dorchester, the
Roman Dorocina, almost at its mouth.   It seemed
appropriate in that ancient town that when I inquired
of a lady of not less than seventy years of age on a point
of local history, she told me that it would be better to
ask one of the older people.

Of the River Thame, Dr Robert Plot, LL.D., first
custos of the Ashmolean and Professor of Chemistry at
Oxford in 1683, tells us that 'the water at Sea, in eight
months' time, acquires so spirituous and active a
quality, that upon opening some of the Cask, and
holding the candle near the bung-hole, its steams have
taken fire like Spirit of wine, and sometimes endanger'd

firing the ship. Hence 'tis also that its stench is no absolute corruption, and that after a third or fourth *fermentation*, it equals the waters of the Well in the Haven of *Brundusium*, and stinks no more; and though the Mariners are sometimes forced to drink it and hold their noses, yet upon that account they do not sicken; whereas all other *waters*, as far as has been hitherto observed, become irrecoverable upon stinking, and dangerous to drink.'

The learned doctor takes his information concerning Brundusium, the modern Brindisi, from Pliny, who in Book II of his *Natural History* devotes considerable space to the remarkable properties of rivers and springs, telling among other surprising facts that a cold spring in Illyria sets fire to clothes spread out above it, that mares pastured on the plains beside the Black Sea suckle their foals with black milk, and that during the last moments of the Emperor Nero rivers were seen to flow backwards. Perhaps the more modern philosopher in gathering his facts about stinking waters suffered also from excess of credulity.

Seen from the Clumps, Dorchester is dominated by its abbey, a great barn-like building, 'made into a noble structure by Normans who followed the Saxons and the English who followed the Normans.' Historic monuments abound within, and a Jesse window expresses in stone traceries the genealogy of Christ. Tablets on walls and effigies in marble and alabaster recall warriors known and unknown, clerical and lay. But not one of them has sadder associations than a plain

slab set in the floor of the centre aisle with this
inscription:

Reader!

If thou hast a Heart fam'd for
Tenderness and Pity, Contemplate
this Spot
In which are deposited the Remains
of a Young Lady, whose artless Beauty,
innocence of Mind, and gentle Manners,
once obtained her the Love and
Esteem of all who knew her, But when
Nerves were too delicately spun to
bear the rude Shakes and Jostlings
which we meet with in this transitory
World, Nature gave way.   She sunk
and died a Martyr to Excessive Sensibility.

MRS SARAH FLETCHER,
Wife of Captain FLETCHER,

departed this Life at the Village
of Clifton, on the 7 of June 1799,
in the 29 year of her Age.
May her Soul meet that Peace in
Heaven, which this Earth denied her.

Sarah Fletcher committed suicide, and according to
the custom of that period she should have been buried
at a cross-roads with a stake through her heart; but
instead her body was given a place of honour in the
abbey church.   Her husband had not only been faith-
less to her but had proposed matrimony to a wealthy
heiress, living at a distance, and had been accepted.

Only at the last moment did Sarah hear of this; only just in time to stop the marriage ceremony did she arrive at the church.   Then she returned to the big seventeenth-century house at Clifton Hampden where she had spent her married life, and with her handkerchief and a piece of 'small-cord' hanged herself from a curtain rod in her bedroom.

The inscription on the abbey floor might reasonably have been the end of this unhappy episode, but that was not to be.   As time went on the big house where Sarah had lived and died acquired the reputation of being haunted.   Tenants stayed but a short time: the garden became a wilderness, the outbuildings fell to ruin. After some years, because of the low rental that was asked, the place became a school, and though the headmaster had heard rumours of eerie happenings he said nothing of them to his pupils.   'There are always noises in old houses,' was his answer to his own questionings.   Then in the early hours of a morning the son of that headmaster, a seventeen-year-old boy who later became the Rev. Edward Crake, heard footsteps in the passage, his door was opened and he could hear the footsteps in his room; but though it was moonlight he could see nothing.   The unseen walker went from the room and the door closed.

The boy said nothing to his parents of what had happened nor of similar occurrences during the night that followed; but on the third night he determined to leave his door open in order if possible to see the originator of the sounds.   And, as he told the story in later years, 'I had not long to wait; the footsteps of someone wearing high-heeled shoes came into my room; they approached the bed and then retreated. I sprang up and ran into the corridor, fully lighted by the moon, and there the figure of a young woman was made manifest to me. She was standing by one of the long windows and she was wearing a black silk cloak; her hair was bound with a purple-red ribbon. There was nothing dead about her; she seemed tremendously alive but her eyes were full of tears.

'The next day,' continued Mr Crake, 'I mentioned what I had seen to one of the assistant masters and found that I had stumbled on what was common knowledge to the staff, though any hint of it had been withheld from the pupils. At a quarter to three every morning restless footsteps wander from the room in which Sarah Fletcher hanged herself.'

The speaker of these words died in 1915, but others of equal integrity, before and since his death, have told of the footsteps they have heard in that house in the early hours of the morning, and of the woman in a black cloak with tangled auburn hair who had looked out at them from noonday shadows or been seen in the half-shades of moontime.

For a few miles below Dorchester the Thames is hidden to view from the Clumps, but beyond Wittenham Woods it reappears on its way to Wallingford. It was at a boatyard not far above Wallingford bridge that I inquired if they had a dinghy for sale.

'Not just now, but maybe later,' said the elderly foreman. Would I leave my address?

'Wittenham, you live at Wittenham? Why, you must know Judge Waters up near Clifton,' he said as I gave him the scribbled information.

'I know him well,' I said.

'Ah, Master Dick, a good lad,' said this veteran of the river. 'I brought him up to the boats. He coxed his college after—that would be about 1898 or '99.'

I thought then of the very old labouring man who had been brought into the court-house in Cork to give evidence. Every question put to him by counsel was answered without hesitation and with clarity. As he was leaving the witness-box the judge complimented him on the way he had given his evidence and asked if he might know his age.

'I'm ninety-two, your honour, and may I ask how old you'd be?' said the old man.

The judge, a trifle taken aback, replied that he was sixty-seven.

'Well, you've got a good job, young man. Stick to it and you'll go far,' said the elder as he left the box.

To return to the boatyard. That foreman had been with the firm, boy and man, for seventeen years when he decided to get married.

'What about a wedding present?' asked the proprietor. 'I'd like to give you some token of the day.'

'Well, sir,' said the prospective bridegroom, 'if I might have one of our skiffs for the day I reckon we'd have a nice honeymoon.'

The wedding morn was bright with sunshine, but before the couple left the church clouds had come over the sky. Just as the flower-decked craft was pushed from the landing-stage and the current had caught the last handfuls of confetti, raindrops plopped in the river. By the time the bridegroom had rowed into the shelter of Wallingford bridge the rain was coming down heavily. He tied the skiff under an arch of the bridge and there they spent their day.

'Couldn't 'a' been a better honeymoon anywhere,' said the bridegroom when he returned to work next morning.

Wallingford, though five miles below Dorchester on the river, is just visible from the Clumps. Proudly the inhabitants of that town claim to belong to one of the oldest boroughs in England; proudly they point to the charter given to them by Henry II.

'Henry, by the Grace of God, King of England, Duke of Normandy and Aquitaine, and Earl of Anjou, to the Archbishops, Bishops, Earls, Barons, Justiciaries, and all my ministers and faithful people in all England and Normandy, French and English Greeting:

'I command you that my faithful burgesses of Wallingford shall have my firm peace throughout my whole land of England and Normandy, in what place soever they be. And know ye that I have given and granted to them for ever all their liberties and laws and customs well and honourably, as well and as honourably as they have had them in the time of Edward the king, and in the time of my great grandfather, King William, and of his son, the other King William, and in the time of my grandfather, King Henry . . . I also grant to them that, wheresoever they shall go for the purpose of buying or disposing of their merchandise, throughout

all my land of England and Normandy, Aquitaine, and
Anjou, By water and by strand, By wood and by land,
They shall be quit of toll, passage, pickage, pannage,
and stallage, from shires and hundreds, and from the
suits of shires and hundreds, from aids by the sheriff and
those serving under him, from geld and Danegeld, from
hideage and Blodewite and bredewite, from murders
and the various consequences pertaining to a murder
. . . Given at Oxeneford, the first of the ides of
January, 1155.'

For the benefit of those who like myself are lacking
in medieval vocabulary, a *pickage* is a duty paid at fairs
and markets for the putting up of stalls and booths; a
pannage is the custom money paid for the running and
feeding of hogs in a forest. *Stallage* is the rent paid by
traders at a fair for permission to show their goods.
Geld is any tax or imposition; *Danegeld* is a tax covering
the finding of soldiers to withstand an enemy, in
particular the Danes. *Hideage* is the tribute raised on
every hide of land, *Blodewite* or *Bloodwite* the compensation paid for the shedding of blood, *Bredewite* the fine
for light weight in loaves of bread. 'Murders and their
consequences' in this connection probably refers to the
pecuniary punishment awarded to those who wilfully
fail to produce a man guilty of murder.

But the history of Wallingford does not begin with
the charter: the remains of the ramparts which still
encircle the town are successors to the more primitive
fortifications of the early Britons. Coins were minted
there from before the time of Canute. William the
Conqueror soon after the Battle of Hastings marched

on the town and forded the river where the bridge now stands; he was met by the Lord of the Manor, who delivered the town into his hands, and later he received the Archbishop of Canterbury, who had come to swear fealty to him.   For both of these occurrences William held Wallingford in high favour, and when in 1069 the curfew was imposed throughout the land, he ordained that in that town it should not be rung till nine o'clock, whereas elsewhere the appointed hour was eight.   To this day the curfew is still rung at 9 p.m., and should any wonder at the seemingly arbitrary length of the tolling they have only to consult their calendars to find that the number of notes corresponds to the date of the month—one on the first, two on the second, and so to thirty-one.

CHAPTER EIGHTEEN

'HOW NOW! a rat?'
I had been telling them in the Plough about a boy in the village who had seen a rat on the river-bank. 'It was sitting up on its hind legs holding an egg in its paws, and another rat was biting its tail,' he had told me.

'During the war, in France,' said Dick Shippon, 'we was billeted in a barn and the rats was there in thousands. An' one night I woke up, 'twas about three in the morning, an' the last quarter o' the moon or thereabouts was shining through a top window and lighting up the rafters. An' there was a big beam running crosswise from side to side of the barn and the light was catching it. And when I look up I seen a rat on it—the queerest thing in all my life. He was moving along on his hind legs and he was holding an egg in his front paws—a hen's egg, I reckon it was, by the size. Yes, sitting up like a squirrel he was, and another rat behind him holding on to his tail, and in front of him was another rat showing him the way, and there was a rat on either side of him kind of guiding him.'

Old Andrew Kirby who lives on the other side of Clifton bridge cut in on Dick. 'Week afore last,' he said, 'there was a big rat come into my yard after a dead chicken. In the full light of day it was, about four o'clock in the afternoon. Bird been killed by a passing car and I'd put 'er for time bein' on gravel heap inside gate. I seen the rat, a proper big 'un. He come over and sniff, and then he goes away. Better bring the bird in, I says, so I fetches it in an' 'angs it in kitchen. Blow me, when I looks out again there's rat and four others with him, all looking around. Of course, they runs when I goes out, so then, just for to see what would 'appen, and maybe get a shot, I puts bird on gravel heap again. Blow me, in two minutes the big rat is back by 'isself, and he sees the chicken and he runs up to it, and then away he goes a second time as if to fetch the others. So I nips out again and fetches in the bird, and then all the rats come back and sniff around looking for it, same as they done before. And then all of a sudden the four smaller ones sets on the big one and kills 'im! Thought 'e been playing 'em tricks, I suppose. Yes, right through the neck they bit him, and left him dead.'

Strange stories, I thought, as I walked home. But not more strange than those recorded by Dr Maurice Burton of the British Museum (Natural History) in his book *Animal Legends*. Among other instances of con-certed action by rats, he tells of a clergyman in West-morland who, after one of his hens had by her cackling announced the laying of an egg, 'observed two rats come out of a hole in the hen-house and proceed direct to the nest. One of the rats then laid down on its side, while the other rat rolled the egg so near it that it could embrace it with its feet. Having now obtained a secure hold of its egg, its companion dragged it into the hole by its tail and disappeared.' This behaviour he corroborates by a similar incident seen by a farmer in the west country who, when asked why he had not tried to kill the rats, replied, 'If you was seeing a queer thing you never heard of avore, *you* wouldn't have killed them rats either.'

Other accounts, fully authenticated, come from places as far apart as Surrey and Sumatra, Bristol and New Guinea, all of them adding emphasis to the summing up of M. A. C. Hinton, who, after many years' study of these creatures, referred to them as 'diabolically clever.'

Wonder upon wonder. I was sitting in my sunlit garden contemplating the creamy blossoms of a Mermaid rose that spreads itself across the west wall of the cottage, when I noticed a bee carrying away from it a scrap of leaf. Looking more closely then at the foliage, I saw that many of the leaves had pieces cut from them on one side or the other of the midrib, leaving holes that in most cases were oval but occasionally circular. And while I was meditating on these the bee returned, settled on a leaf, and in a trice had neatly cut from it a piece similar to the others. As I watched it moving round the preordained shape with the speed and assurance of a tailor's scissors, I could hear the tiny crisp sound of it cutting through the rose leaf.

So this was the leaf-cutting bee of which I had read but never seen—the small solitary that constructs its

egg capsules with fragments of rose leaves, about a
dozen to each cell, oval for the sides, circular for the
ends, all with a fraction of the leaf's serration to
interlock the sections. A hole in the ground or a
crevice in the bark of a tree are its favourite sites for
nesting.

'I will tell you a true and tragic story about that bee,'
said an entomologist to whom I mentioned what I had
seen. 'During the war a squadron of Spitfires was
stationed in Africa a few miles from where I was
stationed myself, and not long after their arrival one of
them crashed soon after taking off. The pilot was
killed and the plane a total loss. Then at intervals of a
few days a second and a third crashed in similar circumstances and it seemed impossible to diagnose the cause.
Sabotage was suspected, and suspicion fell on a young
man whose parents were of enemy origin. He was
court-martialled and found guilty. But while he was
still in custody yet another plane crashed, though this
time it was not so badly damaged as the others and it
was possible to make an examination of the wreck.
In doing so it was discovered that a small inlet pipe
under one wing was partly clogged with fragments of
leaves. Naturally this meant nothing to the mechanics,
but the fragments were handed to a visiting scientist to
see if he could make anything of them. ''Where is the
nearest garden?'' he asked, and was taken to the
officers' mess. There from a rose-tree that grew
against a wall he picked a dozen leaves whose perfora-
tions exactly matched the fragments found in the pipe.
The aperture was of a size well suited to the bee's

requirements, and four times it had tried to build a nest in such a site. As a result four planes had been destroyed and three pilots killed.'

That same entomologist invited me to his home in Oxfordshire. 'You might care to see some moths,' he said. I expected to be shown glass case after glass case of exotic creatures with wings stiffly spread and with pins through their bodies, creatures from tropical Africa, brilliant and bizarre. I did indeed see moths resplendent and fantastic, but they were not in glass cases and they had not come from Africa. They were alive and they had come from the nearby English countryside, and with closed wings were waiting till they could take flight again in the summer's dusk.

My host had on his lawn a contrivance like a dustbin, with a blue electric bulb at its apex. 'Ultra-violet,' he explained; 'I leave it on at night and the moths are attracted. Then they drop through the openings in the cellophane cover'—he lifted the lid—'and I examine them in the morning. That's last night's collection—I kept them for you to see.'

Inside the tub were layers of papier mâché egg trays —'maximum surface area in minimum of space'— and each tray was thickly populated with moths. There before me were scores and dozens of what I had always thought to be rarities. Tiger Moths with their strongly marked black-and-white upper wings hiding the scarlet and metallic blue of underwings and body. Privet Hawks with their four-inch stretch of

clouded wings folded over red-and-black barred bodies. There was an Eyed Hawk with the peacock-like ocelli shining from its pink-tinged underwings, and there were many of the dove and slate grey Poplar Hawks, like large crumpled leaves.

'One night's catch,' repeated my host, 'probably a thousand specimens, probably thirty or forty species.'

What seemed to be a brown beech leaf resolved itself into a moth, the fore edge of its upper wing meeting the underwing like the midrib of the leaf. There were many that might have been twigs of silver birch, and several of a species whose head and thorax resembled polished stone but whose mottled hinder parts of wings and body were like lichen. In all of them the resemblance to their natural daytime background was perfect.

Alfred Russell Wallace, writing of the leaf insect of Java, says: 'It is a common thing for a stranger, when asked to look at this curious insect, to inquire where it is, and on being told that it is close under his eyes to maintain that there is no insect at all but only a branch with green leaves.' And of the wingless stick-insects which are abundant in the Moluccas he says: 'They resemble sticks so exactly in colour, in the small rugosities of the bark, in the knots and small branches imitated by the joints of the legs . . . that it is absolutely impossible, by the eye alone, to distinguish the real dead twigs which fall from the trees overhead from the living insects.'

I had seen stick-insects in Samoa, where they are a pest in coco-nut plantations, and had indeed once owned a leaf insect from Ceylon; but I had never realized that here at home, night after night, flit and hover such multitudes of equally unimaginable perfections.

On the far side of the river, in the meadows below Clifton lock, a massive bull, Old Tom by name, a bit yellow about the shoulders but pedigree Hereford, moves with pasha-like dignity among his cows and their offspring.

'Quiet as a kitten,' said the herdsman when I suggested to him that a bull on a towpath was matter out of place.

A contributor to *Country Life* once said that you can make friends with a bull in his stall merely by scratching him, though he adds that it is wise to leave his head alone and concentrate your blandishments on his stern; then should you chance to meet him loose in a field he will be the more inclined to present that nether and safer end for further attentions. He also remarks that should the animal become temperamental and over-vigorous in his return gestures, as bulls are prone to do, you need only to get a grip on his tail, and as he takes you for a cross-country run steer him to a tree or fence where you can part company on easy terms.

At first glance this advice seems on a par with that given in Samoa to anyone likely to find an octopus in his canoe: 'Bite it between the eyes.' This in fact is the regular *coup de grâce* given to their catch by octopus fishers in those waters, and though I have never tried it myself I have many times seen it administered. Instantaneously, with the first crunch, the writhing tentacles drop from your limbs, limp as spaghetti. Of course, if the bull is by the towpath, you've always got the river.

I had mentioned in that house of comfort, the Plough, that visitors to my cottage were inclined to ignore the knocker on my front door and barge through the garden gate, hoping perhaps to surprise me in my studio surrounded by a harem of models.

'You need a bell on the gate,' said Mrs Sully as she attended to my glass. Then, leaving the bar for a moment, she returned with an ancient copper hand-bell. 'Found it here when we came,' she said; 'you take it home and try it.'

Next morning it was used to call me from my studio. I found my visitor, who had lived all her life in the district, admiring the bell. 'It reminds me of the old sheep bells,' she said. 'I remember when I was a child there was an old ewe with a bell round her neck who used to lead the lambs along the village street to the slaughter. They used to have a lot of sheep in the farms round here then, and the great thing was to have the lambs early in the season, to kill and send up to London. They killed them over at the Plough, in a shed at the back where the kitchen is now. And the ewe with the bell would lead them from the farm, and all the lambs would follow her. And then she'd go back to her farm alone.'

'It has a fine clear note, that bell,' I said; 'it carries well down to the studio.'

'It's a wonder the distance the note of a small bell will carry,' she said. 'I remember our old cook telling me that when she was a girl, lying in bed here in Wittenham, she'd hear the ferry bell at Clifton—that was before the bridge was built in 1865. Sometimes it would be late at night, and she'd say to herself, "That will be the young ladies from the Manor, coming back from their dancing over in Dorchester or Oxford."'

That day was a Sunday, and as the morning hours went by the bells of the village church seemed more and more insistent. Wind's gone to the east, I thought. Then in the late afternoon I heard the singing of hymns, and looking from my gate I saw a procession of villagers led by the vicar and his choir. The day was the Feast of the Dedication of the parish church to St Mary the Virgin, and following a centuries old custom the parishioners were marching from one sacred site, their twelfth-century church, to another yet older, that on which the village cross stands and where about the year 636 a man from Rome named Birinus first spoke to the savages of Wessex concerning Christ.

CHAPTER NINETEEN

ARDEN is a lovesome thing but, God wot, one does need a seat in it. My predecessor bequeathed to me everything that a cottage garden should have, from raspberry canes to a clothes-line, save only a plank where in the cool of the evening I might sit and contemplate and grow.

Then on the day of the expedition to the Windrush, as we drove through the village of Marcham, a few miles west of Abingdon, I noticed a timber yard with a profusion of newly cut boards stacked for seasoning, trees sliced and sliced again from end to end and the slivers piled alternately with transverse battens to let the air pass through. The edges were untrimmed, their outlines with the bark still on were as the trees had grown.

'Just what I need for a garden seat,' I said.

'All sorts of timbers in there,' said Dick Gower. 'Pointer is the name—he'll cut you anything you want.'

So next day I visited Mr Pointer. 'Elm is what you need,' he said. 'Unless you prefer teak. It lasts longer.'

'Elm will see out my time?' I queried.

He checked a ready agreement. 'I wish you a long life,' he said, 'but I think it will.'

'Boxwood is what I'm used to handling,' I told him as he led me through a foam of shavings from which butt ends of sawn timbers emerged like jagged rocks in a rough sea.

'Box is a hard wood,' he said. 'The hardest I touch is an occasional bottom foot or so of the bole of a birch-tree, or a sycamore—just the bottom foot, the rest of them is soft. Of course, it's mainly elm I handle, with a bit of cedar and beech or oak now and then.'

'I have a walnut ready to fall in my garden,' I told him.

'I don't touch it,' he said. 'That's for veneers, cabinet-maker's job. Do you know how thick they put on a walnut veneer? As thick as my thumb nail—no thicker than that. It's just for show.'

A small girl was hovering near by with a large pair of opera glasses in her hands.

'Here, Jane,' called Mr Pointer, 'stop bird watching for two minutes and fetch me that elm bowl from the house. That's my daughter—she's mad on birds,' he said; 'spends her days with her nose in the hedges.'

'Not many birds to watch in the timber yard,' I suggested.

'The place is *full* of birds,' said Mr Pointer earnestly. 'Sometimes it seems that everywhere I look there's a bird building. There's three of them in the laurel hedge now, two thrushes and a blackbird. And last year we had the shed full of them—a thrush in that corner, a jenny wren under the rafter over there, another of them here by the door.' He showed me an old nest tucked behind the door-post, in a crack hardly wide enough for a bee to enter. 'Come, I'll show you my robin,' he said as he led me into a smaller room off the main shed. One wall was lined with pigeon-holes full of all manner of bits of timber and tools. 'There she is, in the end hole. She started building in the one beside it, then changed her mind—I don't know why.   She's been sitting now three days.'

The electric saw started up beside us and I couldn't hear Mr Pointer's voice above the din.   But the robin showed no sign of disturbance.   Then Jane reappeared with the elm bowl and we moved into the open.

'Lovely bit of wood,' said Mr Pointer, taking the bowl and adding to its polish with the palm of his hand. 'Look at it here: rings very close, not much growth, several years' hard weather.   Next two years better, more open grain.'   Then pointing to a sudden and contrasting change in the texture: 'I reckon a neighbour come down here, in a storm or maybe 'twas felled. More light and air makes a wonderful difference.'

How beautiful the grain of timber can be, light and dark streams serpentining and eddying from pool to pool along the plank, traceries that record the life history of the tree, every strain or stress of growth revealed in the rhythm of the fibres.   Where a log has been cut at the junction of a branch there will be a 'curl': where the root of the branch, deep into the bole, has been cut there will be a knot.   In the timber yard they speak of the first saw-cut as the opening of a log; they say that only an expert can predict the patterns that will be found in an unopened log.   Every tree trunk a casket.

The choice of the timber that I needed was not difficult: a board about seven feet long and eighteen inches wide for the seat; another of the same length for the back; and then two shorter and thicker pieces for the sides.

'That seat won't blow out of your garden,' said Mr Pointer as we roped the boards to the car.

When I inquired the price of what I had bought, Bill, a son of the house, did some complicated sums with his finger in the timber dust that lay on a saw table and calculated a price that would have seemed cheap for a gross of matchsticks.

The making of the seat was elementary. Two rectangular slots cut in each of the sides to take the tongued ends of the seat and back, and the tongues bored to take a peg, and the job was finished save for the smoothing of an edge that might have been dangerous to nylons and the rounding of a few corners.

And then I sat back and the scent of new-sawn timber mingled with the scent of new-mown lawn. A thrush was singing from the pear-tree, two goldfinches were searching among the tulips, a sulphur yellow butterfly flittered past, and behold it was very good.

CHAPTER TWENTY

DOWN BY the river the willow catkins are in spume, and the eyot is white with Summer Snow Flakes. Selective by nature, only a few sites please these giant snowdrops, but, as can happen in other forms of life, once the choice has been made restraint vanishes. In this water garden they seek to drown all other growth, even stinging-nettles must struggle for their lives. Only a sprinkling of kingcup gold outshines the silver.

It was after one of the warmest nights of the month that, coming back to my garden from an early morning visit to the river, I found bloom after bloom of irises bursting from their sheaths and spreading petals to the sun. The Snow Flakes had hung their heads, modest as brides beneath their veils: these lustrous virilities were exulting in their glory.

'Stained glass windows we call them,' said the girl who later in the morning brought me my newspaper.

Morning, early morning, that is the time to see and know the river. Often before dawn, in dressing-gown and slippers, I creep down the Green Lane to a gate that opens on to mown grass. There, inside the gate, I leave my slippers, and silently on dewy lawn make my way to the water's edge. The night's last stars are high in the western sky: eastward a thin sickle of the ageing moon loses its lustre in the strengthening promise of day. Birds are still silent; there is no sound but the rustle of the distant weir. Scarcely a movement anywhere, moths pale as comfrey drowse their slow way from plant to plant. Bats only are in haste, whirling specks of blackness, on their aerial excursions.

In my small boat I move up-stream past untilled meadows heavy with resting kine. The white lilies of the stream are still folded, glimmering ghosts of their noonday selves. The yellow lilies, the 'brandy flasks,' more hospitable, are open as flasks should be on occasion, even before dawn. For instance, how can one buy cattle on a road three miles out of Galway at four o'clock on a pitch-black morning in February with rain falling if one hasn't had an introductory nip? I was only there for company, but I recognized the acumen in Jim Moriarty's speech when, after meeting him in the empty square, he suggested that we should open the fair at Kelleher's bar. The trouble at Galway fairs is that though scheduled to begin at 8 a.m., those sellers who get their cattle to the market early are likely to sell quickest, and those buyers who go out on the country roads to meet the incoming animals have the best choice of what they may buy. Fairs are still held on the dates appointed, but if progress continues backwards as at present they must shortly begin and end on the day before. I wouldn't be surprised to learn that many of the discrepancies in our present-day calendar have arisen through similar natural proceedings.

Slowly the promise of dawn spreads upwards in the east and a whisper of wind stirs the unsheltered pools. From a copse beyond the weir come the soft words of ring-doves, and then as I ship my oars and let the boat float with the stream I hear the harsh cluck of moor-hens. Twelve of their nests I had counted by daylight in that short stretch of river, two of them with eggs, a third from which a family had been reared; the others were, I think, spare rooms for the young. All twelve with but one exception were built in the reeds some two feet above water level, and all but that one had leaves pulled down and bent over them to form canopies. The exception was set low among shoots of willowherb.

Now rooks, dark and raucous, are hurrying across the sky and, as if awakened by their chatter, thrushes,

chaffinches, and warblers are muttering and chirping. Moving with the current I pass into deep shadows, and then out again into light-struck waters. Lawns and gardens and tall houses with curtained windows appear. What are they dreaming of, those sleepers in darkened rooms? I wonder what nebulous charades are being played by their unconscious minds?

I remember a dream that came to me towards dawn on a day in March near thirty years ago. It was after I had taken our newly arrived Irish maid to London for the day, not only to visit my wife, there awaiting an important event, but also to see Buckingham Palace. Never mind if Bridie had carried a few dispatches during the Troubles, what she now wanted to see above all else in London was the home of the king and queen. The day proved to be a long one and we didn't get back till late. That night I slept soundly until the twilight hours of morning. Then it seemed to me that I was having tea with Queen Mary in Buckingham Palace, the two of us alone, and just as she had the teapot in her hand and was asking me if I took milk and sugar, a telephone rang.

'Excuse me, Your Majesty,' I said, 'but I think that call is for me. My wife is expecting a baby.'

'Run along and answer it,' said the queen. 'I quite understand.'

So I rose from the chintz-covered arm-chair, to find myself sitting up in bed at home in Berkshire and the telephone echoing from the hall.

'Boy or girl?' I wondered as I ran down the draughty corridor—if a boy we had decided to call him Finnbarr, after the patron saint of my native city of Cork.

'You'll be glad to hear,' said the doctor's voice from London, 'that Finnbarr and Crowbar have both arrived safely—fine lads the two of them.'

CHAPTER TWENTY-ONE

I T IS NICE to sit in a boat near to a lock and listen to the drowsy tumblings of water at the weir. It is nice to sit on a bench in the garden of a lock and yarn with the lock-keeper while he awaits the coming of other craft.

'Yes,' said my friend Mr Sutherby of Day's Lock, by Little Wittenham, one noontime hour, 'in 1923 it was, time of King George V, and he wanted to make a present to the Sultan of Zanzibar. They had nothing but the old stove-pipe weapons out there then, couldn't hit at twenty yards, and we was to present them with a three-ought-three. So our skipper and Jimmy-the-One and a few of us lads took it ashore to present it to the sultan. Little chap he was—well, I'm no giant and he wouldn't come above my shoulder. They'd never seen nothing like this rifle before. So to kind of demonstrate what it would do the gunner's mate sees a gazelle at about five hundred yards and shoots it. Of course the sultan is delighted; nothing would do him but he must have a go too. Well, there wasn't no gazelle in sight for him to have a pot at, so what does he do but point to one of his chaps—one of the Court I suppose he'd be—and tell him to get out there and act as target. It was all our skipper could do to stop it. Not that the chap would've come to any harm, most like.

'There's *Kingfisher II* coming up,' he said as he rose to open the lock gates for a white launch which had

appeared below us.   I followed him to give a hand with
the sluices.

'Nice bit of work that,' he went on, nodding towards
the launch as together we put our weight against one of
the gate levers.   'Built it himself, from stem to stern;
says the only thing he didn't make was the canvas
awning.   He built a trailer for her too, tows her about
the country behind his car—down to the Norfolk
Broads and then up here.   He comes from the north—
proper engineer he is.'

'Not many private launches on the river these days,'
I remarked.

'Mostly hired,' he said.   'All the *Maids* and the
Stars—every time they comes through they got a
different owner.   I know the ships but I don't know
the crews.

'Speaking of that same island, Zanzibar,' he continued when in due course we had returned to our seat,
'we seen one of them religious fanatics being walled up
and   left to die there.   One brick every so often.
Nearly to the top they were with the chap we saw—
just a couple o' bricks still to go—and passing food
over to him.   Oh no, he hadn't committed no crime—
just religion, dunno what kind.'

I asked if he had seen anything of the cloves for which
the island is famous.

'Cloves?   You'd smell 'em ten miles out to sea,
with the wind off shore.   No, I didn't see 'em growing
but I seen bales of them in mats being loaded on to
lighters.   We wasn't watching for cloves—slaves was
what we was after.   Supposed to be all finished, that

trade. Plenty of it still behind the big doors with brass studs—unpaid servants, they call 'em. We had two gunboats in the Persian Gulf to stop the trade—they might as well have stayed in the Thames. I seen one bundle of rags come ashore one day—an old woman, black veil over her face, black everything down to her toes. She had to step from one dhow to another, and I was looking at the reflections in the water. She wasn't no woman; I seen her legs, and a bit more too.'

'Clear water in that harbour?' I suggested.

'We was lying in six fathoms and you could count every link in our cable.'

At another lock the keeper told me of a pair of tree-creepers that had nested in a crevice between the door-post and stone-work of an old barn not far from his house.

'It was last April,' he said; 'not many boats on the river, and I had plenty of time to watch. They collected all their nesting material inside the barn, but they always brought it out into the open by the door, and then they'd run up the front of the post and take it into the chink. When they'd put it where they wanted, they didn't come back outside but went straight through between wall and post into the barn to fetch more; then they'd come flying out by the door and in again to their chink. A proper merry-go-round it was with the two of them working. There was an owl in that barn too,' he went on. 'An old brown one; he'd sleep away the day high up on a rafter. Yes, and he'd come at you in the dark of a winter's night if you were passing with a torch, strike at your head and knock your hat off.   He didn't come out through the door; he came through the slit up high in the gable end. Not more than four inches wide it was, and I've seen that bird go through and you couldn't tell he'd folded his wings with the speed he travelled.   Have you ever seen a bittern?' he asked me.

'Not in this country,' I said; 'but many in New Zealand.'

'I saw one on the Broads in Norfolk last year,' he said, 'and in a manner of speaking if I hadn't noticed it I wouldn't have seen it.   Its head and neck were stretched up straight and it was swaying them from side to side with the squalls of wind as they hit the reed beds.   When the sun came out its throat was yellow as buttercups, and when a cloud came over, the feathers were grey as that T.C. paint—Thames Conservancy, that is.   But 'twas the swaying took my fancy,' he said; 'this way, that way, in time with the stems around it. You couldn't believe it wasn't a bit of the vegetation.'

I told him how I had seen as many as six bitterns at a time on a lake near Napier, and that what had struck me then was the way that at one moment you'd see a bird standing among the reeds, clearly defined, and at the next it would have melted into the background and become invisible.   Then a few moments later it would come into focus again.

'Like fading in and out on the pictures?' he said.

I agreed.

'It's the swaying that does it,' he said.   'Yes, and I'm told you can hear their booming a mile away, but I never heard it.'

'Nor have I,' I said. 'But a farmer in New Zealand told me it sounded like a cow on its back in a drain.'

'Talk of noise,' he remarked, 'we nearly had a launch on its back in the lock this morning. Old fellow with his family, yachting caps and all, never been on the river before—he comes into a full lock and makes fast to the bollards. As the water goes down, over heels the launch. Screech, bellow! If I hadn't closed the sluices quick, the keel would have been looking me in the face.'

CHAPTER TWENTY-TWO

WHEN THE THWART of a boat has lost its resilience and one's stern needs a change of fellowship, it is pleasant to throw anchor ashore and drop in to one of the smaller resorts that occupy strategic points by roadside and river. There are many 'Trouts' beside the Thames, but none with softer seats than in the bar of that small inn by Tadpole Bridge.

'Proper leather they are, those seats,' said Auntie Flo, wife of the proprietor; 'come from the old Clarendon in Oxford, when they knocked it down. There's a Woolworth's going up there now, big as a skyscraper.'

'Did you hear what the men got paid for putting up that scaffolding?' asked one of the two lorry drivers whose vehicles were standing outside. 'Pound an hour, they told me—pound an hour!'

'Well, I reckon they earned it,' said the other. 'They can't stay on that job more'n an hour or two at a stretch, gets dizzy you see, apt to miss a footing climbing about in that web like a spider.'

'You'd see them chaps round the town,' said the first man, 'spending the money as quick as they earned it—a lot of wild Irishmen they were; couldn't get the local fellows to take on the job.'

'And what would you like?' asked Auntie Flo, coming towards me.

'I'd like a large whisky,' I said, for I was tired.

'A double?'

I nodded.

'I'll put in three,' she said.

It wasn't the first time I had visited that house. Indeed, fifteen years earlier I had written of the fish's head which, stuffed and glaring from a shield on the wall, demonstrates that trout have teeth on their tongues.

'Yes,' said Auntie Flo, 'my niece is a liberian; she works at a libery in Nuneaton, and she's always talking about that book of yours.   And when people come into the bar here and ask about the trout's head, I always say, "I don't rightly know but you can read it in that book of his. *He* knows all about it."'

Above the glass case that held a three-pound rudd was a painting of willows by a stream, sensitive in colour and handling.

'My brother did that,' said Auntie Flo. 'He was never like the rest of us; didn't seem to want to settle to nothing, trying this and trying that.   One day he walks into the bar. "Got something for you, Flo," he says, and he hands me that picture.   Never thought

he'd done it hisself—never knew he could paint.   But
it seems he'd been at the painting some time, without
a word about it to any of us.'

As the evening light faded, Auntie Flo's husband
carried in two oil-lamps and hung one over the bar
table and the other in the porch.

'No electric for us,' he said.   'Can't abide it—cruel
bad for the eyes.'

'But wouldn't we bless the man that brought it
here,' said Auntie Flo.

Tadpole Bridge beside the inn might be a child of
Halfpenny Bridge at Lechlade, ten miles nearer to the
source.   The same simple arch, the same atmosphere
of calm about it, the calm of the upper reaches.   Earlier
that day I had been to Rushy Lock, a mile up-stream,
isolated among its meadows, visited only by water-
borne traffic.   The lock-keeper's wife was mowing
the grass in her garden when I arrived: her husband had
gone to do the shopping.

No, I didn't want to come through, I told her, as she moved towards the gates. I just wanted to make a drawing of the little stone bridge across the Sharney Brook that isolated her kingdom still further from the north.

'Yes, we're new to the job,' she said in answer to my question. 'Only came here six months ago and it's our first lock.'

'I suppose your husband's ex-Navy?' I said.

She laughed. 'No, he's ex-office,' she said, 'and we're still surprised.' Then she told me how they had always been fond of the river, taking their holidays in a boat whenever they could, until one day when they were camping her husband said to her: 'I've had enough of office life, what about having a lock?'

'Of course I thought he was joking and didn't think about it again till one evening he came from the office. "They've accepted me," he said. "Who've accepted you?" I asked. "Thames Conservancy," he answered. "What have they accepted you for?" I asked. "A lock," he said; "starting training at Teddington next month."

'Last April they gave us this lock on our own. Got a prize for the garden our first summer. It's all like a dream!'

'What about the winter?' I asked.

'People tell us we'll be cut off from everything when the floods are out, but who cares about that? Not us!'

Yet still higher on the river I spent some pleasant days at the Swan by Radcot Bridge. 'The house is yours,'

said Mr Bowl the landlord, when I put my bag inside his
door. 'You go where you like and ask for what you
want: a couple of extra eggs for breakfast or a pot of tea
at any time. There's boats in the boat-house, help
yourself, and if you want to make a splash in the river
there's deep water under the diving stage by the
bridge.'

I didn't want extra eggs, boats, or splashes; I was
content to sit in the garden and watch, appropriately
enough, the swans, seventeen of them, riding so
proudly the wind-ruffled water, or gliding effortless
where no ripple but of their own making disturbed the
reflected light. Kingfishers streaked up- and down-
stream, swallows splashed as they swooped at drowning
insects, wagtails pied and grey ran to and fro about the
lawn. When I needed a rest from sitting I would
wander along the towpath to the lock and just beyond
it the bent-back wooden span known as Old Man's
Bridge. Big insolent steers in one meadow, in the
next younger cattle more polite, moving aside to let
me pass. Fishermen and fisherwomen all the way on
folding stools, fixed as photographs. Across the river
copses of willows, reed beds, and rushy pools among
intermingling streams and rills, difficult country to
travel for man or beast.

There is little sensation of distance when crossing a
field—one just moves from side to side of it, from
hedgerow to hedgerow, with ever varying footfall, with
ever varying invitation. On a road, whose interest
is merely incidental to its purpose, the same fraction
of mileage seems many times as long. Sometimes

in the fields there is a beaten track, in summer dry and hard as it winds drunkenly from gap to stile; but in winter its inconsequence seems reasoned and sedate, as it skirts the areas of flood water and the pools that well up from sodden soil.

Of all beaten tracks the towpath by a river must be one of the richest in association: in the past hard toil for horses, men, women, and even children; to-day a right of way to 'the width of the waters, the hush of the stream.'

On my first evening in the bar of the Swan, an old man came from his chimney corner and addressed me.

'I wir proper frit when I see you coom in wi' they whiskers,' he said. 'Tho't 'twur my o'd faather coom back. A-ah—eighty-six 'e wur when 'e died—o' course you be younger'n that. Got all stook away wi' 'is water, that's what took 'im. Went a bit light in the 'ead like, at the finish, thinking all the time as 'e wur abedding down the cows.'

We were joined by another elder of the village.

'How you been keepin', Jim?' asked my companion.

'Not too special, Willum,' answered Jim.

''Ad a good 'oliday last week?'

'Wunnerful 'oliday.'

'Where did you go?' I asked.

'I stop at 'ome and got me taters in.'

Mr Bowl passed a pint of mild across the counter to Jim. 'Seen any rabbits?' he asked.

'Not a one in two years,' said Jim sadly.

'Jim doesn't hold with this rabbit disease,' said Mr Bowl to me.

'Took away me trade,' said Jim. 'Couldn't even sell me ferrets—nobody wanted 'em. And look at the vermin now! I seen a fox, eight o'clock this very mornin', walk up the village street. Can't let your 'ens out. And the cats—they used to go out and catch themselves a young rabbit, now they goes for the birds.' He shook his head in disgust, then turned to me. 'Didn't I see you figuring out the bridge earlier 'n the day?' he asked.

'You did,' I said, 'and can you tell me why the arches are so different—the middle one nearly square and the side ones pointed like windows in a church?'

'I couldn't tell you that,' he said; 'that bridge is there years on years on years.'

'One of the first bridges ever built across the river,' said Mr Bowl.

'They reckon 'twer the civil wars,' said Willum. 'Cromwell and King Charles they coom along yer and set into each other. One of 'em—the King, I think 'twer—gets yer first and blows up middle o' bridge. T'other coom along in the night wi' 'is army; they doan't see the 'ole in middle of bridge, 'cause of it being dark, an' two thousand on 'em fall in an' wur drownded.'

'Some say,' said Mr Bowl, 'it was in an earlier war it happened, time of Richard II. One of his generals— Earl of Oxford, I think—fell into the trap and lost most of his men. They say that was how Henry IV got to be king—put Richard in prison and took his crown.'

'We calls that bit of 'igh field yonder across the road the Monument,' said Willum, ignoring the remark.

'Folks do say as 'ow 'twer there as the drownded men was buried.'

Historical discussion was interrupted by a fisherman who brought in a big perch which he had caught that afternoon.

'A present for you,' he said to the landlord. 'Must be near on three pound.'

Mr Bowl ran his fingers over the shining scales. 'We'll have him mounted,' he said. 'We want a perch on the wall. I'll put him between the big barbel and the two bream.'

CHAPTER TWENTY-THREE

THE SWALLOWS observe the time of their coming but who shall number them? The martins also that with beakfuls of mud contrive their nests beneath the eaves of our houses or the arches of our bridges; likewise those birds who from high soaring bring down food to their nestlings within tunnels of sand.

In 1939, passing under Clifton Hampden Bridge, I counted 128 nests of house martins glued to the arches, and recorded the fact in my *Sweet Thames Run Softly*. In the years 1951 to 1954 other observers counted an average of 450 occupied nests under the same arches. During those intervening years the bird population of the bridge had trebled itself, and it has now come to be accepted as the largest colony of this species in the British Isles.

'Where they most breed and haunt I have observed the air is delicate,' said Banquo, telling of 'the temple-haunting martlet.' That bird is known to-day as the swift, but I suspect that what with the hautboys and the torches, the attendants and the distinguished company, not to mention the general tension of Act I, Scene vi, before the castle of Macbeth, the ornithological cerebrations of Banquo may have lacked precision and that the 'pendant beds' to which he referred may have belonged to house martins rather than to swifts. Be that as it may, it seems that the largest colony of those birds visiting our islands has chosen the loveliest stretch of the Thames for their 'procreant cradles.'

As the shank from the cup of a rowlock, so springs the six-arched bridge from its Berkshire foothold. On the one side of the river wide meadows, where coots and moorhens forage and herons cogitate, spread to the water's edge, the level of their flood-inviting banks no more than inches above the summer stream; on the other side trees of infinite variety in form and colour, black and silver poplars, lusty elms and ashes, oaks and chestnuts, screen the three-mile loop of the river's course to Little Wittenham.

The mellow brickwork of the bridge is already a unit of Clifton Hampden village when the arches touch the Oxfordshire bank. If ever cottages could be said to nestle, none could more aptly be so described than this cluster of human habitations that with generations of thatch upon their roofs snuggle into the rising ground which separates them from main roads and aerodromes: cottages where yew hedges, centuries old, present the most futuristic of sculptured forms, where vines tethered to ancient gable beams hint at the hospitality of home-made wines within. As functional as the curves of a living body are the mouldings of the thatch that shelter doors and windows.

'Ninety-four years all but two months we been here —excuse the dishabill,' said Harry Ebsworth as, waving his hand towards a cup and a plate on the table, he drew me into his cottage—first on the left when you turn right over the bridge. For the most part the walls of his living-room were covered with large photographs in heavy frames, but facing the door a dresser held rows of blue willow-pattern plates. Two ginger china cats that smiled from the mantel-shelf seemed to be his only companions.

'That's my dear grandmother, Susan Ebsworth, sir,' said Harry, pointing to a photograph in a massive frame, 'and that's my dear grandfather, Silas Ebsworth,' as he pointed to another framed in the same style. 'He died at the horse's head, sir. Holding them for Mr Noah Paxman, his employer, on a Sunday morning after church. "All right, Silas," said Mr Paxman as he picked up the reins, and down dropped my dear grand-father, dead on the road, before, as you might say, the whole congregation. No, not horses nor wheel, sir— heart, just heart. Yes, my dear grandparents moved to this cottage two years before the foundations of the bridge were laid, and here I was born and here I still live.' He did not mention his parents but I presumed that they also had lived there. 'And that's my dear aunt,' he continued, indicating another frame, 'and that bit of fine stitchery beside it, "Teach me Thy Way, O Lord," is her work. It's got her name on it,

Martha Ebsworth, wove there in the bottom corner, just where it's frayed.   And that's *my* portrait,' he went on proudly, '1914—first day in khaki I had it took.   Of course, they give us Kitchener's blue to start off with.   Ox. and Bucks, 26th Division.   Same as you, perhaps, sir?'

'I was 29th Division,' I told him.

'Three paces to the right,' said Harry with a salute.

I had last seen Harry a few days before, working on the village green in Long Wittenham.

'What about those nettles outside my boundary hedge?' I asked him.   'They could do with a bit of harvesting.'

'After I've had me dinner this very day, sir, I'll be coming to see you, sir.   I needs a stone for my dear sickle.   I needs a nice blade for that job, sir, then I'll slaughter 'em—oh, I'll slaughter those dear nettles, sir!'   And he hit himself a thump on the chest which made him jump.

We moved into his front garden and he told me of the grape-tree that had grown against his cottage.   'A tall and splendid grape-tree it was, sir, right up to the thatch, and the main issue of it as thick as my thigh. But it died, sir, and now there's only the nails that trained it to the wall is left.'

A car pulled up on the further side of the road and a woman, emerging from it, waved to us both.

'Good morning, Digger,' she said, coming towards us.

Harry pulled at a non-existent forelock.   'Good

morning to you, Mrs Merrick, Ma'am. I hope I see
you in very special health.'

'The snapdragons are doing well, I see,' said Mrs
Merrick.

'Those dear plants of yours, Ma'am,' said Harry,
'I give them a drink every single day, no matter
whether there's rain or no.'

Mrs Merrick had stopped to offer me a lift back to
Wittenham.

'Why the name "Digger"?' I asked her as we drove
homewards across the bridge.

'Nobody knows. He doesn't know himself,' she
said. 'He got the name in the war and it's stuck to
him. Now he digs graves for the village—perhaps
that's why he calls everything "dear," he's got so in
the habit of being sympathetic.'

My conjecture of a misnomer for the swift by Banquo
was strengthened when I chanced upon a similar confusion on the part of Gilbert White who, in a letter to
his friend Daines Barrington, wrote: 'I sit down to give
you some account of the house martin or martlet.' And
consulting the *Shorter Oxford Dictionary* of 1939, I found,
'The Martlet is in fact the Swift, though formerly often
confused with the Swallow and the House Martin.'

But what an astonishing knowledge of birds and their
ways did Shakespeare possess, and how often and how
splendidly did he use that knowledge in metaphor and
allusion.   Unlike the later poets. he did not address the
birds directly: instead, he used them to illuminate his
own sequences of thought.

The crow doth sing as sweetly as the lark
When neither is attended, and I think
The nightingale, if she should sing by day
When every goose is cackling, would be thought
No better a musician than the wren.

Though 'good faith, I am no wiser than a daw'
before the 'full-winged eagle,' I am sorry that Shakespeare allowed Iago to speak slightingly of the snipe,
for of all the sprites of bog and moor none has more
charm of eerie cry or elfin flight. Perhaps the poet
took a cue from his contemporary Drayton who, born
but a year earlier and in the same county, wrote of 'the
witless woodcock and his neighbour snipe.' Why
Drayton should have disparaged the woodcock also I
cannot understand. Had he never seen the flight of
the bird among trees? Had he never observed the
behaviour of the bird with its young? It has now been
established definitely by the British Trust for Ornitho-
logy that the parent woodcock carries its offspring from
place to place between its thighs. Only a little while
ago, when wandering in the valley of the Tay, I saw in the
woods near Ardeonaig two dark specks crossing the
road ahead of me. Before those specks had reached
the cover of long grass I had time to recognize them as
a woodcock and its chick, the parent bird walking
with its long bill held vertical to the ground. Together
they hurried into the undergrowth on my left and I
thought that I had seen the last of them; but a moment
later the adult bird appeared on the road again.
Standing up to her full height, she flapped her wings

ostentatiously to distract me from her chick—I could
see the silver of the underwings shining in the sunlight.
Afterwards she flew across the road and into the cover
from which she had first emerged.   Several times I
saw her peeping at me from behind bracken and fern,
and I wondered if there were others of her brood that
she wished to lead across; but if that were so she had
counselled them to lie still, for I saw no sign of them.
Then a second time she walked across the road before
me and into the wood where she had left her solitary
chick.   The little one was waiting for her, and together
they vanished over the rocky bank of a small but deep
streamlet.   Nothing witless about that behaviour.

I am sorry also that Shakespeare's one mention of the
wagtail, in *King Lear*, should have been contemptuous,
for whether grey, pied, or yellow, few birds of our
countryside do so invite the human heart to dance.
And the mallard, so splendid on the wing—surely his
looks are warrant for his gallantries: Falstaff of all
people to be a judge of valour or of virtue!   And while
presumption is upon me, let me suggest that a pipit
would have been a better simile on the two occasions
when the sparrow is referred to as host of the cuckoo
(in *Lucrece* and in *Lear*).   In the collection of 165
cuckoos' eggs of which I have spoken earlier, there
were but five sparrows' nests, whereas there were fifty-
seven of the pipits, twenty-four of the wagtails, and
thirty-nine of the various warblers.

CHAPTER TWENTY-FOUR

FROM THE house martins under Clifton Hampden Bridge it is but six miles up-stream to a colony of four martlets who for many centuries have roosted heraldically on the shield of Abingdon Abbey: *Argent, 4 martlets between a cross fleury sable.* Why martlets? I wondered, until I remembered the medieval belief, still surviving in many parts of Britain, that the swift has no feet and never comes to earth. In Wales when, on a summer's evening, I watched a number of the birds spiralling upwards until they were lost to view, I was told that they spend their nights on the wing in the upper airs, and recent scientific observation suggests that this is true. What better symbol then to accompany the cross than these earth-free spirits? To this idea an historian answered no. The martlets, he said, are from the shield of Edward the Confessor, who liked Abingdon so much that he kept 'hauks and hownds' on the meadows by the river that he might have sport with them when on his frequent visits to the town.

But might not my conjecture still apply, even if indirectly? Might not Edward, whose virtues were those of a monk rather than of a king, have chosen the soaring martlet as his symbol? Our word is derived from the French *martelet*, the swift: Edward was by birth, upbringing, and disposition more Norman than English.

In another connection the martlet is borne in

heraldry, as a mark of cadency, on the shield of the fourth son, to denote that even if a property can be divided between the first three sons of a family it is unlikely that there will be anything left for a fourth, and it is better that he should take wing and not return, seeking his sustenance elsewhere.

The abbey was founded in A.D. 675, and according to Hilaire Belloc 'it is not fantastic to compare its religious aspect in Saxon times over against the King's towns of Wantage and Wallingford to the larger national aspect of Canterbury over against Winchester and London.' Speaking of it in relation to Westminster and Chertsey, the two other great Benedictine foundations of the same century, he says that of the three 'in a way it is the greatest, for, without direct connection with the Crown, by the mere vitality of its tradition, it became something more even than Chertsey was, wielding an immense revenue, more than half that of Westminster itself, and situated as it was, in a small up-valley town, ruling with almost monarchical power.'

Another historian, a late colleague of mine at Reading University, Sir Frank Stenton, wrote: 'It was from Abingdon rather than from Glastonbury that the new monasticism of the tenth century derived its distinctive features. The cathedral church of Winchester was colonized by monks from Abingdon; and at Winchester, in a synodal council summoned by King Edgar, the rule developed by Ethelwold at Abingdon was formally promulgated for acceptance by the monasteries of the Benedictine order throughout England.'

In the suppression of the monasteries by Henry VIII, Abingdon was the first of the larger foundations to be dissolved. On 9th February 1538 the abbot and his monks signed a deed of surrender to the king, yielding to him all the lands, buildings, and possessions of their ancient house. Within a few weeks the great church had been stripped of its ornaments and much of it pulled down. In less than half a century it was a complete ruin. Yet there is still an Abbot of Abingdon, for the Roman Catholic Church, not recognizing the Reformation, confers that title on the vicar of the Church of St Paul near the Vatican.

To-day little remains of the whole institution but the gatehouse and a fragmentary range of secular buildings which include the thirteenth-century 'Checker Hall' and the late fifteenth- or early sixteenth-century 'Long Gallery,' with unglazed windows continuous along its northern wall. Of the hall itself there is written evidence that it was used not only as the Exchequer, that is to say, the central counting house of the abbey, but also for the safe keeping of the archives. There is evidence too that its finely vaulted undercroft was the abbot's wine cellar. Impressive within for its proportions and for the remains of its stone-canopied fire-place, it is for the 'hooded' chimney-stack of that fire-place that it is of interest without. Claimed to be 'the finest of its kind in the kingdom,' of dressed and undressed stone, it rises high above the roofs to termi-nate in four gables, each pierced with triple lancet openings as though they were the windows of an anchorite's cell. Whatever the original uses of the

'Gallery,' and there are many conjectures, its beams are superb in the simple significance of their forms and pattern.

The ground where church and cloisters stood is now a public garden with flower-beds leading the eye across green lawns to ivy-bound fragments of traceries and pillars. No need here for artificial incongruities to add interest to the vistas: each time-weathered stone is a granule in the architecture of history.

Never an Abbot of Abingdon, though born in the town, Edmund Rich became Archbishop of Canterbury in 1233, and a few years after his death in 1240 was canonized St Edmund of Abingdon. It is told of his early days that on one occasion as he travelled towards Abingdon he saw at sunset a flight of black crows, which he recognized immediately as a swarm of devils come to carry away the soul of a local usurer, and sure enough when he reached Abingdon he found that that rapacious man was dead. It is told of his later years that he always wore the cheapest of grey or white tunics in preference to 'purple and fine linen,' and that even when he was Primate of all England 'he did not blush to take off his own shoes.'

For over a thousand years the history of Abingdon has been linked with the history of England and its kings. The first recorded royal visit was in 871 when King Alfred, fresh from his victory over the Danes at Essendune, came to the town and, wishing to reduce the power of the abbot, 'took away violently' from him the township and many other possessions. More pleasant was the later visit of Canute, of ocean fame,

who brought with him a reliquary of silver and gold and
two bells as a present to the abbey.   The fact that
many military tenants of the abbey had fought in the
Battle of Hastings did not endear it to the Conqueror,
and in the early years of his reign the church was
plundered of its ornaments; but when in due course the
abbey came under the jurisdiction of a Norman abbot
it enjoyed William's favour and prospered greatly.
He, his rough son Rufus, and the gentler Henry (afterwards Henry I) paid many visits to the town and
enjoyed the hospitality of the royal palace built three
centuries earlier by King Offa, of dyke fame, on the
island which lies between the two channels of the
Thames at the southern approach to the town.   In
parenthesis, it was during the reign of this Henry that
Geoffrey of Monmouth, drawing on Bede, Nennius, and
a rich imagination, created for us the legend of King
Arthur and his knights.

During the Civil War, when Oxford was the Royalist
capital, Abingdon became a much contested strategic
point.   More than once Charles I held a council of
war in the Bell Inn, now known as the King's Head and
Bell.   Charles II in the course of a royal progress in
1665 spent a night in the town which is said to have
cost the inhabitants the equivalent in modern money of
'tuppence on the rates.'

Three years later that same king's Surveyor-General
of the Victualling Office, formerly Clerk of the King's
Ships, later Secretary to the Admiralty, by name
Samuel Pepys, spent a night in the town where, as he
recorded in his diary, 'had been a fair of custard; and

met many people and scholars going home; and there did get some pretty good musick, and sung and danced till supper.'

The fair of custard to which he refers was not one of the many festivals for which Abingdon was noted. Originally of devout intention, though later become secular in character, the fairs were instituted in honour of the saints with whom the town had particular associations, the two most important being St Mary's Fair in honour of the Blessed Virgin, patron saint of the abbey, and St Edmund's Fair, in honour of that local saint. A scholar has suggested that by 'fair' Pepys meant 'fare,' adding that the word custard in those days also signified pastries or fruit pies for which the town was famed.

Pepys was not the first literary figure to enjoy the hospitality of Abingdon, for of John Skelton, created Poet Laureate by both Oxford and Cambridge, who was 'educated and broughte up in Oxfoorde,' we read that 'on a tyme he had been at Abbington to make mery, wher that he had eate salte meates, and hee did com late home to Oxforde, and he did lye in an ine named ye Tabere whyche is now the Angell, and hee dyd drynke, and went to bed. About midnight he was so thyrstie or drye that hee was constrained to call to the tapster for drynke, and the tapster harde him not. Then hee cryed to hys oste and hys ostes, and to the ostler, for drinke; and no man wold here hym. Alacke, sayd Skelton, I shall peryshe for lacke of drynke! what reamedye? At the last he dyd crie out and sayd: Fyer, fyer, fyer! when Skelton hard every man bustle hymselfe upward, and some of them were naked and some were halfe asleep and amased, and Skelton dyd crye: Fier, fier! still, that everye man knewe not whether to resorte. Skelton did go to bed, and the oste and ostis, and the tapster with the ostler, dyd runne to Skelton's chamber with candles lyghted in theyr handes, saying: Where, where, where is the fyer: Here, here, here, said Skelton, and poynted hys fynger to hys moouth, saying: Fetch me some drynke to quenche the fyer and the heate and the drinesse in my mouthe: and so they dyd.'

To counterbalance these associations of literature with moistness, we owe to Abingdon a volume dry as a mummy but no less valuable, 'A CLASSICAL DICTIONARY: containing a copious account OF ALL THE PROPER NAMES mentioned in ancient authors; with the Value of Coins, Weights, and Measures used among the Greeks and Romans; and a Chronological Table, from the Creation of the World to the Fall of the Roman Empire in the West, and in the East,' by John Lemprière, D.D., who was headmaster of Abingdon School from 1792 to 1810.

As I finished transcribing this impressive title, my eye wandered onwards over the chronological table. Twenty-four pages of mind-shattering events authoritatively dated, from the creation of the world in 4004 B.C.

The Deluge, I learnt, occurred in 2348.

The Tower of Babel was built in 2247.

Joseph was sold by his brethren in 1728.

Moses was born in 1571.

Helen was raped by Theseus in 1213 and fifteen years later by Paris.

Saul was made king over Israel in 1095.

Elias the prophet was taken up into heaven in 896.

The Sabines were raped in 750.

Jerusalem was taken by Nebuchadnezzar on the ninth of June 587.

Jeremiah the prophet died in 577.

Mahomet I, in his 53rd year, flew from Mecca to Medina on Friday, 16th July A.D. 622.

And so continues the chronicle for eight centuries more, until as a finale the taking of Constantinople by Mahomet II in A.D. 1452.   Then follows a list of forty of the most learned men who lived in the fifteenth century, among whom were Chaucer, Gutenberg, Thomas à Kempis, and Savonarola.

In my copy, immediately under that chronology, there is pencilled in boy's writing:

> R. J. Lee   born 1873
>   ,,   ,,   went to school 1879
>   ,,   ,,
>   ,,   ,,

Though space was left for other events in his career, they were never filled in.   Was Lemprière too much for the poor little fellow at six years of age?

CHAPTER TWENTY-FIVE

TO THE STRAINS of 'Roses of Picardy' played by the steam organ of a merry-go-round, two men carried a crate of live ducks along the bank of the brook that flows through the village of Grove. It was eight o'clock on 'pinning up night' of the village feast and the last event was about to take place. Several hundred people had deserted the swing-boats and the coco-nut shies, the shooting galleries and the dodgems, and had gathered by the short stretch of river between the two bridges of the village. Six men, stripped to the waist, were standing on the parapet of the upper bridge ready to jump at the blast of a whistle and chase the duck that had been put into the water some hundred yards down-stream. The whistle sounded, the men leaped and plunged and struggled to where the duck itself was splashing with delight in its native element after spending most of the day in a pen. It was only when the leading competitor had got to within a few feet of the quarry that, startled from its ablutions, the bird took to spattering semi-flight down-stream. But by then it was too late, for the athlete, throwing himself as a footballer might do, caught the duck in a low tackle. That bird became his property, and though he might compete again he could not win another.

'You can't chop your Momma up in Massachusetts,' blared the organ, and as if inspired at the thought of choppers the second duck gave of its sporting best.

Hither and over and through and among its would-be captors it wheeled and splashed and dived, until a youth with the speed of a wing three-quarter caught it at the touch-line.   Race followed race on much the same pattern.

'A pity it's a cold night,' said a man beside me, 'or we'd have had the ladies in too.   You should see 'em! Some of them young and some of them old, and some of them dressed and some of them half dressed.'

'And some of 'em near *un*dressed before the race is finished,' added another.

'How long have these duck races been going on?' I asked.

'Two hundred years or more, I reckon.   I'm an old man but I remember my father saying *he* remembered his grandfather talking about it.   Said it was started by the Bay Tree, that pub by the bridge there.   Nowadays it's the football club as runs it,' and as he spoke I heard a collecting-box rattling behind me.

Then, as aspirants for the last duck lined up, one of them, who had already tried repeatedly but with no success, tore off the legs of his trousers, and leaping into the water in the briefest of shorts scored immediate victory.

A fortnight before the duck races at Grove there had been a 'Donkey Derby' at East Hendred, a few miles to the east, in which the animals were ridden by professional jockeys from nearby training stables.   Several of the donkeys refused to move from the starting post until their jockeys dismounted and pushed them from behind; one of them at the sound of the whistle bucked its rider over its head, another had to be towed by spectators to finish the course.

As traffic daily frets the simple contour of a bridge, so the bare windswept sky-lines of the Berkshire downs are often broken by strings of racehorses out for exercise from their stables in the valleys below. Rarely now do we see a horse harnessed to plough or wagon; the animal, even in our own life's span, has become a creature bred for sport and pleasure, or to enhance our occasions of ceremony. Anthropologists tell us that it was first domesticated in Persia some six thousand years ago, and then chiefly for religious or aesthetic reasons; only later was it trained to serve. Now released by the factory siren from the rigours of labour, it is again bred for human delight, a delight that has become a cult of almost religious intensity.

So it seemed to me when I attended the Arab Horse Show at Roehampton. There, lovely as the first horse which leapt into being when Poseidon struck the ground with his trident, was the pure white Naseel,

prince of all Arab stallions in Europe. He had come
from Ireland, where he is 'head man' in his owner's
stable, to attend the show, not as competitor but as
guest of honour, and to greet him had been gathered a
dozen of his famous progeny. Did he not in 1951
break all known records by being the sire of the
Champion, the Reserve Champion, and the Runner-up
of all Arab horses shown at the International Horse
Show at the White City, as well as the Champion
'Pony of the Year,' Reserve Champion, and Runner-up
at the 'Horse of the Year' Show at Harringay? Every
one of his numerous children without exception has
been a prize-winner, whether from a pedigree mare or
one of less distinguished breeding. Twenty years of
age, yet as spirited, gay, and proud as any of the younger
animals that paced that well-groomed turf. His eyes
still have the stallion's sparkle, his small ears the
alertness, his neck the strong crest, his coat the lustre
of horses half his age.

As ballet to barn dancing, so are the paces of this race
apart, the source of all stamina in horses, the fastest of
all natural breeds, seeming to skim the ground rather
than touch it as they move. All shades of chestnut,
gold, and bronze, all shades of dappled grey, their coats
with iridescent sheen, their tails arched as those of
satyrs on a Greek vase. Cream-coloured manes lay on
chestnut necks like ash-blonde hair on sunburnt girls.

Strange contrast, I thought, the park-like green acres
on which those animals now stepped, with 'the empty
waste' that is their racial home—'the great barrenness
of gravel stones,' as Doughty describes it, where dawn

after dawn discovers the same arid wilderness and 'no sweet chittering of birds greets the coming of the desert light.'

Doughty in his travels through Arabia rode mostly on camels, 'silent great shuffle-footed beasts,' but a phrase of his prose describes the natural beauty of these horses. Of some passing Arab horsemen he writes: 'Under the most ragged of these riders was a very perfect young and startling chestnut mare. . . . Never combed by her rude master, but all shining beautiful and gentle of herself, she seemed a darling life upon that savage soil not worthy of her gracious pasterns.'

'A Khalif sent his servants to choose him a horse saying: "You know a well-bred pedigree Saluki and the points that govern speed and endurance—look for these points in the horse."' It seemed appropriate that in their own ring near the parade ground of the horses there should be on show close on a hundred of these Salukis or Gazelle hounds. Tall lean animals, hounds of the chase, graceful and gracious, their ancestry of even greater antiquity than that of the horses. There is a tradition among the Arabs that it was Ishmael, son of Abraham, who caught and tamed the first wild horse of the desert. But in a recently discovered tomb that scientists compute to have been an ancient monument in the time of the patriarch, *circa* 2000 B.C., there has been found beside the remains of a boy of fifteen the perfectly preserved skeleton of a dog that was almost certainly a Saluki.

CHAPTER TWENTY-SIX

WHAT WITH the duck races in the stream, the Arabian horses at the show, and a wealth of happenings by the river, I had forgotten the July splendour of country hedgerows. It came back to me one warm and sunny day as I stepped the mile of open road between the villages of Little and Long Wittenham. For a while my thoughts had been cast down by the poignancy of the war memorial, to the one man from that smaller village who had lost his life in the First World War. A lonely road to heaven without a neighbour by his side, I mused; a lonely road to travel for a boy of nineteen, but a longer one for his mother who still lives there to mourn him. Here, on this track, he had looked his last 'on all things lovely'; the same fields ripening to harvest as I saw them, the same profusion of

wild flowers starring the verges.   He too would have
seen the gold of yellow-hammers in the sunlight, the
white rumps of wheatears as they flitted from post to
post of the fence, the rainbow glints of butterflies;
above them all the flocks of peewits circling high.
Butterflies whose days of life are but moments in our
human reckoning, lapwings whose years at best are
scarce a dozen: the life span of a bird, I thought, till I
too end my song.

Just then a small boy raised his cap politely as he
overtook me on his diminutive bicycle.

'Give me a lift, Philip,' I called to him in joke.

He stopped his machine, dismounted, and turned to
meet me.

'I'm awfully sorry, sir,' he said, 'but my back tyre is
nearly flat and I don't think it would carry you.'

My mood was changed.   Here was youth and life
again.   And now the wings of the small and large
copper butterflies seemed more highly burnished, the
powder-blue of the chicory flowers melted into a
tapestry of yellow agrimony and cornflowers, on warp
and weft of green.   At every yard new motifs, new
textures; purple loosestrife beside rosebay willowherb,
russet spikes of sorrel amid purple and golden vetches.

Tortoiseshell butterflies were sunning themselves on
the road, their wings when closed matching its freckled
surface.   One of the rare 'commas,' so like a tortoiseshell but for the scalloped edges of its wings, sat wide
open on a nettle leaf.   Marbled whites flitted to and
from the heads of thistles and knapweed, known also as
the Greater Centaury.   It was with this latter plant

that Chiron, the centaur, salved his wound after being struck in the foot by a poisoned arrow from Hercules. What times those half-horse boys of Thessaly did have, with all the speed of four legs and the convenience of a pair of arms.

Tall racemes of toad-flax, like delicate snapdragons escaped from a garden, topped the neighbouring bed-straws, plantains, and wild pansies. Old folks say that an infusion of those yellow toad-flax flowers is a wonderful application for complaints of the skin.

In the meadow beyond the comfrey-laden ditch a red-legged partridge dodged from one tussock of grass to another. When later in the day I mentioned having seen the bird to an old man who had been a game-keeper, 'We don't want 'em,' he said; 'they drive the others away. Never go in coveys, just one of 'em at a time. They lay in other birds' nests, too. When we used to find the eggs we destroyed them. And when we was on a shoot and we put up a red-leg and he was missed, ''Go after him, Henry,'' his lordship would say to me, ''we don't want no Frenchies here. I likes France,'' he'd say, ''but not the Frenchies' partridge. O' course,'' he says, ''the red-legs isn't French at all, it's on account o' the red trousers of the French soldiers they gets the name.'''

Grasses beyond number wove themselves into minia-ture glades wherein were things creeping innumerable: woodlice, of which there are thirty-seven species in Britain, snails of which there are almost as many, and spiders of which fifty species can be found in any one district of England, of which more than five hundred exist in Britain. Some of the woodlice were the size and colour of a wheat grain; others, darker, shone like steel armour. I noticed one of the smaller ones with the edges of its mantle light in colour, a sign that a moult was imminent: soon it would be finding itself a retreat where, after emerging from the old skin, it could hide, as its relations the lobsters do, until the new chitinous protection had grown. Bright snails with purple bands on yellow, white, or rufous shells, infinitely varied, stretched their delicately tapering bodies, probing and gliding from leaf to leaf. Silver moths were sleeping. Non-spinning spiders were scurrying.

That evening in my garden I marvelled at the plants self-sown in most incongruous places. Unlawful urchins, children of the sun, welcome as mushrooms on the lawn. Great spires of yellow mullein dwarfing the foxgloves, and foxgloves dwarfing poppies and lupins and larkspurs, all of them wantoning in ordered beds. A cluster of columbines entirely hid a stone step. Eschscholtzias and marigolds exulted from crevices in wall and paving.

It might seem from this that my garden is neglected, but far from it; these uninvited, unexpected guests are those that have a more innate aesthetic judgment and a surer knowledge of their own requirements than I possess. As impromptu parties are often the most cheerful, so are 'self-sowns' often the most gay.

In London I had but two window-boxes; now I have a garden. The sun sets and thrushes are active on the lawn. Overhead swifts flying high scream as they pass.

Roses and stocks and phlox, sleepy from the sun, shine with sensuous colour, the cold vigour of the morning light forgotten.   Lobelias in the shadow glow deep as darkest amethyst.   As the petals of crimson flax and yellow rock roses fold upon themselves, those of the pale night-scented stock open to perfume the air.

'Life is very sweet, brother,' wrote George Borrow.

'To be alive is the prize above all prizes,' wrote Llewelyn Powys.

Borrow's *Lavengro* was published when its author was forty-eight, with thirty years of life before him. Llewelyn's words were written at the age of forty-eight when he had but seven years left to him to glimpse the 'unfolding scroll without an end and without a beginning.'

CHAPTER TWENTY-SEVEN

IF I HAD allowed my studio to be tidied the greater part of this chapter would never have been written, for then I should not have found some long-lost notes linking Cork with Australia when in fact I was looking for some notes connecting Seneca, the Roman philosopher, with the White Horse of Berkshire. Things lost through one's own lack of system can be found eventually, but those put aside by others who have a system—never. It is like looking for a book in the British Museum Library from a shelf reference in the Bodleian.

Of Seneca the thought had occurred to me that it may have been with some of *his* money that the great White Horse of Wessex was cut in the downs. We know that this Stoic philosopher was also a money-lender, and we know that he lent money to Boadicea while her husband Prasutagus, King of the Iceni (pronounced Ikny) was still alive. Prasutagus and his war-like tribe inhabited Norfolk and Suffolk at the time, and their chief occupation was horse breeding. As the name suggests, it was they who built the Icknield Way, that great road from Norfolk even into Cornwall, which passes under the very nose of the White Horse. Might it not have been a whim of that warrior queen to cut an emblem of her tribe just below what may have been one of the tribe's outlying fortresses? Might not her husband have refused her the money for the project, saying that he had better uses for it? Might she not then have thought of borrowing for her purpose?

Of Cork and the Antipodes I have surer knowledge. History relates that between one and two o'clock on the morning of 22nd July 1797, Miss Mary Pike, a wealthy Quaker heiress then staying with friends a few miles from the city of Cork, was handed a note from her family physician, my antecedent and namesake Dr Robert Gibbings, saying that her mother was critically ill and needed her immediate presence. Miss Pike dressed quickly and set off for Cork in a carriage lent to her by her host, but she hadn't gone far before she was stopped by armed highwaymen. They cut the traces from her horses and ordered her to move into their own chaise that stood near by. The frightened girl, doing as she was bid, was astonished to find awaiting her the sister of Sir Henry Brown Hayes, a man she had met but once. Still more astonished was she when one of the highwaymen took off his mask and disclosed himself as Sir Henry, and he a former sheriff of the city. She was carried to his home where, with attendant minister and almost at pistol point, she was constrained to go through a ceremony of marriage. Strangely enough, Sir Henry enforced no marital rights, and two days later Mary was rescued 'unhurt' by her friends. Then it transpired that the cleric who had performed the ceremony was no cleric at all, and that the letter purporting to come from my ancestor was a forgery.

As a result of the escapade Sir Henry was compelled

to go into hiding: he was declared an outlaw and an offer of £1,000 was made for his apprehension. Yet in no time at all he was back in Cork and showing himself publicly as if nothing had happened. This went on for nearly two years before public opinion strengthened against him and he felt that it was time to stand his trial. Then, being of a generous nature, he visited his hairdresser, and in words to this effect said to him: 'You have had the care of my head for many years and now there's a thousand pounds upon it. Here I am, give the information and get the money, but don't forget that some day I may be asking you for a share of it.'

Sir Henry was arrested and the hairdresser, Mr Coghlan, got his money and built three brick houses with it. Judge Day, another family connection on my mother's side, presided at the trial. I refrain from the verbosities of counsels Curran, Hoare, Goold, Townsend, Burton, Waggett, and Wilmott for the prosecution and Quinn, Keller, White, Grady, Fitzgerald, Hitchcock, Franks, and Dobbin for the defence; but it is told that on the last day of the trial as Curran was about to enter the court-house an old fishwife, who sympathized with the innocent maiden, called out to him: 'Long life to you, sir, and I hope you'll win the day.' 'If I win the day,' answered Curran, 'you'll lose the knight.' He did win the day, but 'twas only a twilight that followed. Sir Henry was condemned to death but recommended to mercy: his sentence was commuted to transportation for life.

His next outlook on the world should have been

through the barred port-hole of the convict ship *Atlas*, but Sir Henry had lived near Blarney, and very soon he was dining with the captain of the ship and viewing the ocean from the quarter-deck. This of course gave rise to jealousy, which afloat and later ashore gave rise to incidents. But Sir Henry, gallant knight that he was, survived these vicissitudes, though his name in the historical records of New South Wales seldom appears without the accompaniment of trouble. Eventually he became owner of a property near Sydney which is known to-day as Vaucluse, 'an area of 22 acres, 3 roods, 10⅘ perches,' proclaimed a public park on 24th April 1941. Many of the trees which now adorn that park are of Sir Henry's planting, for among the documents relating to the estate there is a receipt for 'Seeds of Trees' among which are included 'One gallon oak, One gallon ash, One gallon beach, One quart anonymous.' More important, however, than the presence of these trees is the absence of snakes, and this also is due to Sir Henry. Knowing that since the time of St Patrick no serpent could live in Ireland, he arranged with friends in Cork to send him five hundred barrels of Irish soil. Then on a St Patrick's Day he assembled a gang of convicts, Irish to a man, and with their help dug a trench six feet wide and two feet deep around his house and filled it with the sacred earth. Tradition says that from that day for a hundred years no venomous creature was ever seen within the circle. If since then an occasional snake has been noticed in the precincts of the house, it goes to show either that even the best soil needs an occasional top dressing or that the activities of earthworms have been all that Darwin claimed for them.

Sir Henry received a full pardon in 1812 and returned immediately to his native city, where in 1832 at the age of seventy he ended his days, in the words of the local paper 'most sincerely and universally regretted, . . . a truly adherent friend.'

CHAPTER TWENTY-EIGHT

I T W A S on a day in August that I set out to visit my
eldest son, who had lately acquired Monkey Island,
in the Thames near Bray.   How would I make the
journey? he had asked: fifty miles by water, thirty
miles by road.   To travel from one point on the river
to another by means of tarred roads seemed con-
temptible.   'I'll come by water even if I have to
swim,' I told him.

The river-steamer left Clifton Lock at noon.   Not a
cloud in the sky, a light wind freckling the water.   We
passed under Clifton Bridge with its nest-corbelled
arches; then almost under the small church on the cliff,
in whose burial ground lie the bones of Sergeant Dykes
of the Grenadier Guards, the man who fired the first

shot at Waterloo and that by accident. They say
Wellington was none too pleased, but that later he
relented and forgave the man.

Three miles of shimmering water to Day's Lock—
three miles of river-banks, with on the one side tall
elm-trees and ashes spreading wide their branches, on
the other side loosestrife and willowherb fringing the
low banks.   Large golden and small blue dragonflies
hover and flit among the purple blossoms.   Here a
water vole is swimming among rushes, there a Little
Grebe low in the water hurries to cover.   Like the
pochard, the tufted duck, and no doubt many other
water birds, the Little Grebe or dabchick when danger
threatens has the power of swimming at a lower level
than normal.   I have seen a cormorant when harassed
by gulls swim with scarcely more than its head and neck
out of the water, its back almost flush with the surface.

Fishermen on stools drowse over their rods; young
men and maidens, old men and matrons, drowse in
camping punts, for the sun is hot.   White swans cease
their preening to lead their smoke-grey cygnets from
one reed bed to another, as proudly as if no one else had
ever been a parent.   From a wide 'heron-priested'
meadow seven great birds rise and flap in heavy flight
to a neighbouring field.   A week before I had seen
them there when soon after dawn I passed in a smaller
boat on the same course.

The river divides, and bearing away from the stream
marked DANGER the steamer moves slowly along the
narrower channel towards the lock.   There on the
bridge above the grey timbered gates appear the white

cap and blue uniform of Mr Sutherby as he opens the sluices to fill the lock and let us enter.

We move in: the gates behind us close, the sluices ahead are raised, and slowly we sink to five feet lower in the world. As we wait for the outpouring, the keeper calls to the skipper of our vessel: 'See those oak baulks on the quay? Pulled up yesterday, sixty-seven years in the water and the adze marks sharp as to-morrow.'

'What you going to do with them?' calls the steward.

'Firewood,' says Mr Sutherby; 'they don't last long once they're dry again.'

He moves towards the long gate lever ahead of us on the right, and presses his stern against it. On the left two children and an elderly man are already pushing theirs against its counterpart. Never at a Thames lock is there lack of volunteers eager to lean against the balance beam that will open or close the highway. Passers-by, passers through—few incidents on their journeyings give greater satisfaction than the swinging of a windlass that will set the Thames a-belching and a-gurgling, or the shoving at a timber that will open the gates to other levels of adventure.

Only a few weeks earlier in Lechlade, higher up the river valley, I had been questioned about that lock. It was as I was walking down the main street that I was stopped by the owner of a small hardware shop. He was extremely stout and completely bald and his presence filled the narrow doorway of his emporium. He held up his hand as I approached.

'Excuse me, sir,' he said, 'but you are an unusual looking gentleman and I like to see unusual looking gentlemen. It's all that hair about your face, sir, that gives you the look. Now I've got no hair on my head or my chin and I reckon I look unusual. That's why I don't use hair restorer. Come inside, sir, I'd like to show you a drawing I've got of the river. Well, it isn't strictly speaking a drawing, it's a print—an engraving they calls it.'

Everything from spades, forks, and garden shears to assorted nails and bottle-openers were displayed in his shop.

'I used to have cigars,' he said. 'I think I've got one now and I'd like to give it to you if I can find it. They don't keep very well.' He pulled out drawers that held screwdrivers, bradawls, and gimlets; he opened glass-topped cabinets that held razors and razor-blades, household knives, forks, and spoons.

'Can't think where I put that print,' he said. 'Had it for years. Day's Lock in 1880—you'd remember it then.'

'Before my time,' I said.

'No, no,' he answered, '1880—you'd remember, you must 'a' known it then.'

'Nine years before I was born,' I told him.

He looked at me a little reproachfully. 'Ah well,' he said. 'Now as to that cigar, I think it must be with the chisels and gouges.'

It was. He produced it, dry and peeling.

'I've had it two years,' he said. 'Now you have it. When I seen you comin' down the street, I said,

"That's the man for my cigar." You have it, sir, and welcome.'

Again our bow ripples the water, and we leave behind us clusters of reeds that sway to the tide of our passing.

The river makes a sharp turn, close by a field of mustard that lies under Little Wittenham Wood. Shining yellow now, when it has withered to mottled brown it will make good outside cover for the pheasants. In some parts of the country mustard is grown for ploughing in as green manure, but here its service is to the birds. 'They get half their living from it,' the gamekeeper told me. Scarcely a hare in that wood nowadays, though formerly there were many from harvest time till leaves had fallen. 'Too much undergrowth for them now. Used to have a couple of woodmen there the whole year round, not one these days. Hares don't like all that tangle.'

On our left the harvest fields are ripe for cutting, tawny wheat, pale silvery oats and barley; beyond them Dorchester Abbey like a great barn dwarfs to toy dimensions the farm buildings around it.

The steamer slows as we approach the triple twist of the river above Shillingford, where low water meadows are dappled with piebald cows. Through the main arch of the bridge we go, and then past courts and parkland, through Benson Lock and on to Wallingford. Here, as at Shillingford, it is not those for whom the bridge was built, the travellers by road, who see the happiest aspect of its lines, but those who view them from the water—great buttressed arches in the middle

stream, lesser vaultings on the bordering banks, still slighter arcs where the flood levels rise to higher ground.

On then five miles to Cleeve and through the Goring Lock. Meadows all but level with the stream are followed by thickly wooded hills. Among the reeds and water plants that fence the open river moorhens cluck instructions to their youngsters hidden under lily leaves: where banks are broken great black-and-white cattle knee-deep in the water huddle as close as piglets on a sow. Under the overhanging many-coloured branches of the Coombe Park woods, mallard in eclipse splash and hide.

These are the waters which for a time during the

Second World War I helped to preserve from enemy attack.   In the first world conflict I had been a captain of infantry, giving in the course of four years' service but one order of significance, 'Cease fire!'—and that after a false alarm.   This time I was captain in the Navy—Home Guard River Patrol—uncommissioned. My second in command was an elderly professor, my ratings were two youths; my vessel was a small open launch with an armament of one rabbit rifle and three rounds of ammunition.   The protection of the lock at Goring and the railway bridge at Basildon, a mile lower down, were my chief responsibilities.   'Don't inquire too closely of the occupants of camping punts: watch only for anything suspicious on the banks,' were the orders from my chivalrous 'admiral.'

Apart from the trains that passed over, the only sign of life that ever I saw near the bridge was a hedgehog which night after night came shuffling along the tow-path.   On the other hand stern duty did once overtake me at the lock.   There, unknown to the enemy, I had established my headquarters, and there at two o'clock one morning the telephone rang.   'An unexploded bomb has fallen in your area: please make contact with it.'   A pretty thought at that hour, with the palest of moons and the thickest of mists. The youngsters were asleep, the professor and I were on watch.   'I will go,' I said bravely, picking up the rabbit rifle, the three rounds, and the chauffeur's cap that had been served to me as naval uniform.   The old man tried to smile as I went out into the night.

Goring and Streatley lie one on either side of the

river. With an instinct akin to that of travellers who believe that the other side of the island is always the most romantic, I crossed the double wooden bridge, hearing the roar of unseen weirs on either side of me.

Streatley was silent and deserted. I stood alone, scarce able to discern the outline of a huge tree that loomed out of the mist. Then suddenly I heard a sound, a sound that might have been a footstep. I listened and heard it again. It came from behind that tree. Here was action, enemy action—parachutist following an unexploded bomb.

With my rabbit rifle at the ready I crept forward, cautiously stalking. As I neared the tree I heard yet another step and I knew that the enemy was there. Then suddenly a shout: 'Hands up!' as a weapon was pressed against my stomach.

'Who are you?' asked a voice fiercely, in unmistakable English accents.

'Home Guard, Navy—who the hell are *you*?'

'Home Guard, Army,' was the reply.

Next day other troops found the bomb, still unexploded, five miles from Streatley.

CHAPTER TWENTY-NINE

As the steamer neared Pangbourne, where the wind plays in the willows, I thought to myself that here must roam the spirits of Mr Toad, Mr Mole, and Mr Rat, for though these children of Kenneth Grahame's mind grew into existence at Cookham Dene, they would surely have moved up-stream with their author when he came to live in that cottage by the church at Pangbourne.

They are not the only literary characters associated with this village, for just over a century earlier Mrs Grundy was born there, her begetter the playwright Morton. In his play *Speed the Plough*, one of the characters, a farmer's wife, is constantly worried as to how this prudish, convention-ridden woman will react. 'What will Mrs Grundy say? What will Mrs Grundy think?' The lady never appears on the stage, leaving playgoers to their own imaginings of her bombasined person. Heaven knows she has not been backward in making her presence felt ever since.

At Mapledurham, three miles further down-stream, I could see from the river the tall chimneys of the splendid Tudor mansion where Alexander Pope grew to love a daughter of the house—the beautiful Martha Blount. Many a time he must have sat with her under the huge cedar-tree that spreads its shadow on the lawn beside the house, and many a time counted the hours with her on the sundial that still stands but a few yards from the tree. Together or accompanied by her sister Teresa they would have wandered in the beech woods that screen the house from northern winds, or visited the old mill beside the lock and listened to the music of weirs and of wheels that even then had been turning for centuries.

Knowing of the poet's crippled body, knowing the tenor of so much that he wrote, I expected to find in his portrait the features of a man embittered and morose. But in the painting that hangs beside that of the two beautiful sisters, in the great panelled hall with its heavily moulded ceiling, he appears as a young man whose features are as full of charm as his hands are sensitive. Yet the love that was in his heart for well-nigh forty years never reached fulfilment: both he and Martha died unmarried.

Long years of waiting had a happier conclusion at Shiplake, nine miles further down-stream, where, after fourteen years of loving, Tennyson was married to Emily Sellwood. The dresses and the cake did not arrive in time for the ceremony but what matter? Like Alf the waterman who, because the day was wet spent his honeymoon under Wallingford bridge and thought no end of it, Alf the poet said it was the nicest wedding he had ever been to.

The seat beside me on the steamer had been vacant for some time when at Henley a middle-aged man came aboard and took his place there. As we cast off from the landing-stage he leant towards me and said with a smile, 'Not many Amblyrhyncus about here!'

'Many what?' I asked.

'Amblyrhyncus—*Amblyrhyncus cristatus*, the big lizard from the Galapagos. Last time I seen you you was drawing him in the British Museum—ground floor, in the reptiles.'

'I remember,' I said; 'and you were in charge, and you lent me your chair because the animal was low down in its case.'

'That's right, and then we had a bit of a chat.   Of course, I seen you about the place a few times before that.   First time you was upstairs with the armadillos, making sketches, and next time you was downstairs with the flamingoes.   Thought to myself, "That's one of 'em all right."'

'A flamingo?'

'No, no, an artist.   I collect artists—not pictures, just artists—the ones I meet.   Don't want signatures, that's kid's game.   I like to meet 'em, have a word with 'em, find out how did they begin.   I'd like to 'a' been an artist—mess about now sometimes with a few colours.   It's the kids I'm keen for.   Got three of them.   I'd like one to get going.'

I told him that my drawings had been for engravings in a new edition of Darwin's *Voyage of the Beagle*.

'Books, books!' he exclaimed.   'I collect them too, in a kind of a way.   Don't read 'em, can't afford that— just read about 'em.   *Literary Supplement* of *The Times*— that's my paper.   That's reading, every word of it! Comes out Fridays.'

I told him that I also took that supplement and enjoyed it.

'You know it?   Why, you're a book man too.' After a pause he went on, 'I seen a book in Oxford last week.   Plates!   Never seen such pictures—show you all the veins in your neck and the nerves in the back of your hand. But twenty-seven bob! Can't afford that— got three kids.'

Now the skipper appeared to check my friend's ticket and to remind us that we were in the famous Henley Regatta reach and that the small island ahead of us, known as Temple Island, was the starting-point of the races. The temple-like building on it had been constructed as a fishing lodge for Fawley Court, the big house on the left, he told us: it used to belong to Major Roderick Mackenzie.

'I knew him,' I said, 'and I've stayed in the house. He had fine things in it. One of the big rooms had hand-painted wallpaper from China.'

'All that's finished now,' said the skipper. 'The place is a school. But there's another temple,' he added, 'on an island further down—Monkey Island at Bray.'

'And that's where I'm going now,' I said. Then I asked if anybody lived on Temple Island nowadays.

'There was an old lady lived there alone till a few years ago when she died,' he said. 'A wonderful old lady she was too, eighty years of age and used to row up the mile to Henley every Saturday to do her shopping. One day in winter when the flood was up, the agent from the Fawley estate thought he'd better go over to the island to see if she was all right. Well, with the way the river was running it didn't take him more than ten minutes to get down to the island from the bridge, but he was a good hour rowing back against the flood. But that old lady, she rowed herself up just after him and it took her no more than half an hour.'

As the suspension bridge at Marlow hove into sight, I saw coming towards us a mahogany launch with two golden cockers sitting up in wicker chairs as if they owned the vessel. A nice harmony of colour, I thought, as I wondered why the set of those dogs' ears seemed familiar. Then I noticed the fair hair of a child who was standing at the wheel: something familiar about that too, I thought—not surprisingly as she turned out to be my grand-daughter. With her, sitting astern, were her parents and they had come to meet me. So at Marlow I transhipped and sailed in style over the remaining eight miles to Bray.

In the year 1738 Charles Spencer, third Duke of Marlborough, bought the eyot known to-day as Monkey Island and built there for himself a fishing-lodge. Having completed the construction of the building, he employed a French artist, Andien de Clermont, to decorate the domed ceiling of the entrance hall with frescoes of monkeys in human dress diverting themselves in human activities, a theme for which the artist

was well known in this country and in his own. The
frescoes to-day are dark with age and varnish, but one
can still see the little animals in elegant dress disporting
themselves. One of them with a beard sits in a boat
smoking, while another in feminine dress ferries him
across the river; a fisherman with a long rod lifts a fish
from the water; a sportsman with a gun has just shot a
bird which is falling through the air. The fishing-
lodge became the nucleus of the present hotel; already
in 1878 it was known to 'boating gentlemen' as a
'house of entertainment.' To-day my son and his wife
enjoy doing the entertaining, as they enjoy residence in
the Duke's other pavilion on the island, known as the
Temple, now a 'place of historic interest.' I visit
them occasionally to admire their walnut-trees and to
advise on the aesthetics of their wine list. That
evening with a few friends we discussed Le Montrachet
'52, Corton Pougets '47, and Corton Grancey '29,
and found nothing wanting.

But gracious and noble as were these wines, the out-
standing event and comfort of my visit was that I fell in
love. That has happened once or twice before in my
life but never with a black girl. Love hits you when
and where you least expect it. Such gaiety and pretty
prattle she had: dark eyes with milky whites, long ears
that splashed in her food bowl as she drank, and the
silkiest of coal-black hair—this daughter of Charybdis
who with her sister Scylla had met me in their launch.
'Cribby,' though golden, had been mated with a black
and had produced seven youngsters all as black as my
shoes, and when I first saw them about the same size,

though more highly polished.   That was why when Diana, my daughter-in-law, said: 'You need a girl about the house,' and put the child into my arms, I knew that all my resolves concerning pets had melted.

What would the woman who had argued about the robins have to say? I wondered, as I travelled home by train, carrying a basket which might have held a pint pot.   That evening as I walked from the post office with a black bundle of inconsequential nonsense, not for posting, under my arm, I felt like the Pied Piper of Hamelin with the troupe of children that followed me. While I had waited for Mrs Cross to slice some of her home-cooked ham the news had gone out, and from far and wide children had come bringing their own furry animals to greet the new arrival.   What was her name?   Was I going to christen her? they asked.

'My Jacko is alive,' said Richard, aged seven, as he worked the fingers of his monkey glove.   'Can he be godfather?'

'My Rosalind is alive, too,' said Lily, aged eight, as she pinched the sides of a piebald oddity and made it squeak.

I had in fact decided to call the pup Tai-lua, but just then that would have required too many explanations. It was the name of a black-haired child in Samoa who was as much at home in the lagoon before her door as in the stream that flowed into it from the hills behind her home.   The name signifies 'two tides,' and it seemed appropriate to one whose vocation was to be a water dog.   If for a few days it applied in rather more local circumstances, that was no concern of visitors.

At my gate she and I parted company with the children, and the first thing she did when inside was to flounder into the half-inch of water that lay in my bird bath, a wide pottery dish that I had brought from Italy.

'Tai-lua is your name,' I said, without benefit of clergy.

CHAPTER THIRTY

A springful of larks in a rolling
Cloud and the roadside bushes brimming with whistling
Blackbirds and the sun of October
Summery
On the hill's shoulder.

SUMMERY it was, at last, in October, with the
sun on the hill's shoulder—the long-embattled
hill of Sinodun that overlooks so many windings
of the Thames. Summery it was in the valleys
where farming men strained to redress their earlier
frustrations, and in the gardens too where polyanthus
and primroses bloomed a second time, and cold-pent
rosebuds burst into gaiety and fragrance, and cabbages
—January King and Christmas Drumhead—as if eager
for immolation belied their names.

Dylan Thomas wrote his 'Poem in October' on his
birthday, his 'thirtieth year to heaven.' The fourth of
that month was for me the first anniversary of my happy
return to the life of fields and growing things. True, I
had spent awhile in islands of perpetual harvest where
seasons are unknown, but there the ground beneath my
feet and all that it produced were strange and un-
familiar. Now I was back on soil not greatly unakin to
that whereof I was born save only that on it tractors
had replaced horses and horses had replaced donkeys.

The turn of the season was celebrated locally by the
World Ploughing Contest, an international event held

for the first time in England, at Shillingford on Thames. Three hundred and fifty acres of land set aside for a hundred and fifty competitors from a dozen countries to prove their skill in turning the sod, either by horse or tractor-hauled plough.

To see each ploughman adjusting the various parts of his equipment was a revelation of the nicety to which this most primitive of implements has been brought. Again and again ere the competition began horses were stopped in their tracks while a nut was loosened to alter the level of a wheel, the angle of a coulter, the set of a point on its share. Only by such finesse could furrows be turned of an even depth and width, each one curling over neatly on to its neighbour and leaving no gaps.

Similarly with the tractors that like an army of tanks lumbered on to the parade ground in single file, their colours not muddy as in war-time camouflage but with the gay contrasts of medieval heraldry—*Azure*, *Gules*, and, sad substitute for *Or*, canary yellow. Racing cars in the pits could scarce have had more subtlety of adjustment.

But for me the horses held the most attraction. What greater prompting to meditation at any time than the sight of a team in a field, turning the soil of a past reaping for the seed-time of another harvest? Here were a dozen pairs with their teamsters, crossing and recrossing the sunlit stage.

Watching beside a man in breeches and leather leggings, I remarked on the prettiness of the newly turned ridges, more closely set than where the machines had been at work.

'Yes, you can't beat the "high cut" for looks,' he

said, 'and it takes a good man to do it well. Not much of it to be seen nowadays; some say its days are finished, no business to be here. Of course, present times, there's not much sowing by hand, and that's where the "high cut" came in—nice sharp ridges with the grain falling in the narrow furrows and the harrow taking the top off the crests to cover them.'

Bowler hats and highly polished riding-boots had been the order of the day at the Arab Horse Show: here among the shires it was rubber boots, corduroy caps, and hats of weathered tweed.

'I think you're Irish,' said a man to me as I was admiring a pair of Pedigree Suffolks resplendent with brasses that told of former triumphs.

'What gives me away?' I asked.

'The tilt of your hat,' he said. 'I can always tell an Irishman—he just sticks it on his head and forgets it. Look at some of these fellows—caps, hats, pulled up here, pushed down there—self-conscious all of them. Look at those two fellows in the pork-pie hats—I wouldn't trust that one on the right, he wears his too straight, has to—it's psychological.'

'Bishops wear their hats straight,' I said.

'Same idea,' he answered. 'Suggests the narrow path, only *they* keeps to it.'

'You don't wear a hat yourself,' I remarked, looking at his wind-blown hair.

'No,' he said, 'makes me look silly—gives the show away, see!'

He laughed, patted me on the arm, and disappeared into the crowd.

A few moments later he was back. 'Beatty would never have won the Battle of Jutland if he'd worn his cap straight,' he said.   Then he disappeared again.

Yet another important anniversary was celebrated in October, the three-month birthday of my merry pup Tai-lua.   Trained to the house at that age—what human child could claim as much?   Able to climb my ladder-like stair, and to make the return journey as if on skis.   Expressing herself now by licking rather than biting.   No need to use a towel below the knees after my bath: each morning she would be there ready to minister unto me as the otters had ministered unto St Cuthbert, licking him dry after his nightly vigil in the North Sea by Coldingham in Berwickshire.   I do not wish to drool, yet even Queen Victoria on returning· from her coronation laid down her orb and sceptre that she might accept the greeting of her spaniel, Dash. Most of us are scarce fit to have opinions of our own but, heaven be praised, we are still low enough in the scale of evolution to have unreasonable emotions.   It was no doubt under the stress of such a one that when in the village post office on Tai's birthday a friend inquired of me about my daughter, I surprised him by replying that she was growing wonderful feathers on her legs.

The more I see of that pup the more I appreciate the benefits of a limited vocabulary.   With one look she can express more than a page of print.   After she and I had occupied my studio for three months without interference, someone decided that its floor should be swept.   Apart from an odd speck of dust in the robin's footprints, the ash of an occasional cigar beside my table, and some straws from Tai's bed scattered here and there among the half-gnawed bones, the concrete might have been a dance floor.   She and I were on a short walk when it happened.   Reaching home, we made our way down the garden path, me on the path, she on the garden, and through our own ever-welcoming door.   One step inside and we both stopped and looked at each other aghast.   There wasn't a bone in sight, not a straw outside her box.   I was speechless. 'My heavens,' said Tai, 'who the divil has been in here?'

She jumped up on to a stool beside my table.   'How have they left that?' she asked with an anxious look, but she had seen for herself and didn't need an answer.

Down again and under the carpenter's bench.   She peered at me from behind some boards that had been stacked against the wall.   'All the chips and sawdust gone!'

Then at the double over the coal-bucket, knocking down my gum-boots which had been placed neatly beside it.

My page of print is exhausted and I haven't said the half of what Tai expressed in a matter of moments.

CHAPTER THIRTY-ONE

I F SUMMER had been tardy, autumn was precocious. While yet we waited for an afterthought of warmth, young blackbirds with rufous heads and dappled breasts pecked at fallen pears; meadows were button-badged with mushrooms, and where there was stubble partridges ran and called. Little stubble in the fields nowadays, with the 'combines' cutting off hardly more than the tops of the stalks and the farmers burning what is left. With each day's ebbing of the sunlight, books were moved nearer to arm-chairs and arm-chairs nearer to the chimney corner.

Long ago I had read *The Travels of Sir John Mandeville*, that imaginary compilation of incredible phenomena by the Frenchman Jean d'Outremeuse, but I had never read the journal of Friar Odoric, one of the narratives on which the Frenchman fed his imagination. Now, while local conversations concerning the number of partridges available for this season's slaughter were still in my mind, I read on the first page of the friar's journal an account of his arrival at Trebizond on the Black Sea, 'a place right commodiously situate, as being an haven for the Persians and the Medes. . . . In this lande,' he writes, 'I behelde with great delight a very strange spectacle, namely a certain man leading about with him more than foure thousande partriges. The man himselfe walked upon the grounde, and the partriges flew in the aire, which he ledde unto a certaine castle called Zavena, being three days' journey distant from Trebizond. The saide partriges were so tame, that when the man was desirous to lie down and rest, they would all come flocking about him like chickens. And so hee led them unto Trebizond, and unto the palace of the Emperour, who tooke as many of them as he pleased, and the reste the saide man carried unto the place from whence he came.'

I read on, and within a few pages reached Chaldea and passed the tower of Babel, thence through many lands, each with its many wonders, to an island 'wherein men and women have dogs faces,' and from there to Ceylon, where there are 'fouls as big as our countrey geese, having two heads.' No small surprise to me when immediately following the mention of such prodigies I came upon the author's solemn assurance, 'I, before Almighty God, do here make relation of nothing but of that onely, whereof I am as sure as a man may be sure.' Then launching forth again in his narrative he tells of a mountain in China over which he travelled, 'upon the one side whereof I beheld al living creatures to be as black as a cole . . . howbeit, on the other side of the said hil every living thing was snow white.' In Tibet he found the women of the country with 'two teeth in their mouthes as long as the tuskes of a boare.'

How was it, I wondered, after reading a final asseveration of his truthful speaking, that a man eminent for his ascetic sanctity, living on bread and water, going barefoot and wearing alternately the hair cloth and a shirt of mail, could offer to his readers such manifest untruths? If in his lifetime men were more credulous- than we are to-day, that was no reason why he should have indulged their fancy.

Then as I pondered I called to mind other incredible stories told by men of equally high endeavour. Can we believe that St Pachome, living in the desert, had only to summon a crocodile as one hails a taxi when he needed to cross a river? Or that St Colman had a pet fly which, while the saint was reading his holy books, would trot up and down the codex ready at any time to keep the place marked with its foot should the holy man be interrupted in his studies? Can we believe the story told of St John when on his second journey from Laodicea to Ephesus? I quote from the Apocryphal New Testament, recently translated by Dr M. R. James.

'Now on the first day we arrived at a deserted inn, and when we were at a loss for a bed for John, we saw a droll matter. There was one bedstead lying somewhere there without coverings, whereon we spread the cloaks which we were wearing, and we prayed him to lie down upon it and rest, while the rest of us slept upon the floor. But he when he lay down was troubled by the bugs, and as they continued to become yet more troublesome to him, when as it was now about the middle of the night, in the hearing of us all he said to them: I say unto you, O bugs, behave yourselves, one and all, and leave your abode for this night and remain quiet in one place, and keep your distance from the servants of God. And as we laughed, and went on talking for some time, John addressed himself to sleep; and we, talking low, gave him no disturbance. But when the day was now dawning I arose first, and with me Verus and Andronicus, and we saw at the door of the house which we had taken a great number of bugs standing, and while we wondered at the great sight of them, and all the brethren were roused up because of them, John continued sleeping.   And when he was awaked we declared to him what we had seen.   And he sat up on the bed and looked at them and said: Since ye have well behaved yourselves in hearkening to my rebuke, come unto your place.   And when he had said this, and risen from the bed, the bugs running from the door hasted to the bed and climbed up by the legs thereof and disappeared into the joints.'

Are the strange phenomena recorded by Friar Odoric the hallucinations of extreme asceticism, akin to the 'holy inebriation' of religious ecstasy spoken of by St. Augustine—we know that lack of certain vitamins in a man's diet can affect his mind—or did he misunderstand or accept too easily what was told to him? Simple men tend to be gullible, and even scientifically trained anthropologists can be taken in by obliging subjects of study who tell them what they wish to hear. Perhaps some of the exaggerations, as when he saw 'mise as bigge as our countrey dogs,' may be mere metaphor and not intended to be taken too seriously. I remember that one day after I had returned to university life from my voyaging on the Thames, I happened to be sitting near the Vice Chancellor at lunch. 'Were you much bothered by rats?' he asked.

'Heavens, yes,' I said, 'rats as big as cats.'

'Gibbings,' he said, 'you are exaggerating.'

Odoric had with him on his journey an Irishman by
name Friar James. It is possible that he of northern
Italy may have taken too literally a few of the descrip-
tions of his companion from further west.

Sir Henry Yule, scholar and commentator, writing in
1866, suggests that some of the more incredible figments
in the text may be due not only to errors of the scribe,
who wrote from the dictation of the friar on his sick-
bed but also from the carelessness of subsequent
copyists. In Tibet, he says, the women wore boars'
tusks as ornaments about their head and neck, and
many of that country's goddesses were portrayed with
two such tusks as teeth: it would not need much
confusion of thought on the part of the redactors to
arrive at the statement attributed to the friar.

Of the two-headed birds in Ceylon he surmises that
they were hornbills, and that the long bill with the huge
casque might well have given a wrong impression, and
he compares the friar's account written in 1330 with
that of Vincenzo Maria, who in 1672 describes a bird
'as big as a goose but with two beaks, the two being
perfectly distinct; with the upper one he croaks, with
the lower he feeds.' And in 1796 the Padre Paolino
speaks of a bird 'as big as an ostrich' that lives on high
mountains where water is scarce and uses the second
beak as a reservoir for a supply of water.

Are these other fantasies concerning the saints mere
wishful thinking, and is it the penalty of our human
reason that facts are not enough for us and that we
clutch at unreason to supplement reality? Be that as it
may, whatever the cause and however much such tales

may strain our credulity, they are precious to us if only that, as Dr James suggests, 'they record the imaginations, hopes, and fears of the men who wrote them; they show . . . what ideals of conduct they cherished for this life, what they thought they would find in the next,' to which I would add ideals also for many people to-day.

This summer six robins have fed from my hand. Would that one hare might come into my garden and give me similar trust.

CHAPTER THIRTY-TWO

Nov_OVEMBER, the second November since I
came to live in the village. The excitement
in the garden that first winter had been
largely one of questioning expectancy: what
was to be my spring and summer heritage of leaf and
petal? This year as I looked at the close-cut stubble in
herbaceous borders, at the grass and bare earth where
bulbs would bloom, at the beds of roses and carnations
smelling only of compost, I knew what I might hope
for. Tidying the old shaggy leaves from the iris plants
I found the fans of young shoots already breaking from
the corms and remembered the wild exultant incandes-
cence of their blooms in May and June. A frost had
crumpled the leaves of the hydrangeas but new sharp
buds were on the stems.

In the fields the green of autumn-sown wheat and
oats was again marbling the soil, and the rhythm of the
hedges had turned to scarlet and crimson. By the
river snipe had returned to feed among the cattle-shorn
rushes, and moorhens were once more sociable of
disposition. Lapwings in their winter assemblies
wheeled above the yellowing elms.

During the summer months dredging machines had
been at work, and on both banks of the river great heaps
of shell and gravel glittered dry and sterile. Behold,
there had come out of the firmament two great claws
that descended into the river-bed and gathered up the
life that lay therein, casting it upon a waterless plain

that it might perish.   Mussels, infinite in their number, snails infinite in their kind, cockles and limpets, mottled and veined, perfect in symmetry; shrimps also and leeches amid the larvae and pupae of insects innumerable, all thrown to wither in wind and sun. So might it have been scratched in gastropodic script on the inside of any shell.   As the Flood that covered but the lower valley of the Tigris and Euphrates was thought by the Sumerian people of that region to have destroyed every living thing from off the face of the whole earth, so might this minor cataclysm have seemed to those more lowly inhabitants of the Thames.   Thinking on these things and of our own short range of vision that credits no coherent thought beyond the world on which we live, I remembered the words of Littré, the French philosopher, to Flaubert: 'Oh, my friend, man is an unstable compound, and the earth a very minor planet.'

And then, as if to disperse such solemn meditations, a flock of domestic ducks came sailing down-stream— Harry Chambers's ducks that he had had to leave behind when he went to live near Oxford.   Though merry enough just then, they too had experienced an emotional disturbance.

'I'll miss those ducks,' said Harry to me on one of his last evenings as landlord of the Plough.   'But I can't take them with me—they wouldn't be happy without their river.   The very first thing in the morning, when I go down to open their pen, away they go to the water and I don't see them again till I call them in the evening.'

'Don't they lay out then?' I asked.

'Oh no,' he said, 'they'd never do that. If one of them forgets before she leaves in the morning, she always comes back. Yes,' he mused, 'I'll miss those birds. One gets fond of them, and they get fond of you. The other day I said to my wife: "Let's take the boat out; we mayn't have another chance." So we got into the skiff and I began to row down towards Clifton. Do you know, at the first bend, just there by the Manor, we met our own ducks! Oh, they were so pleased to see us; they came all round quacking and splashing. Of course, it was new for them to see *us* on the water.'

From among the shadows of a weeping willow, I watched the flight of a cock pheasant as, crossing the river, it whirred low over the shrivelled thistles and teasels on either bank. Though the action of its short rounded wings was rapid, the movement of the long tapering body was like a glide as it touched down into the field where cattle were resting. Friesians, black and white, their markings perfect for engraving: if only the richness of their milk equalled its profusion, the breed would rule the world of market-place and meadow.

Then my glance reverted to the nearer bank and I saw to my astonishment a small lean man come up out of the reeds as if emerging from the river. He carried in his hands a long trident, and when he reached dry ground he hurried towards the nearer of two tall poplar-trees that stood on the bank and hid it among

the branches. From there he moved quickly in the
direction of the further poplar and I lost sight of him.

Not venerable enough for Father Thames, I decided,

but maybe one of his attendants. It was evening and the sun was near to setting. What might not now emerge from those gently moving waters, on whose surface floated the tokens of summer's gilding?

Nothing happened; it rarely does. Yet when I stepped from under my concealing boughs and looked into the foliage of the poplar-tree, there was the trident hanging among the leaves. The handle was not as straight or polished as those depicted by fanciful artists and the three prongs were bent. End of the season, I concluded: even the regalia of river courts must need refurbishing. Perhaps towards midnight I would hear the hammering.

And then a human voice said to me: 'It might be wise for you to take with you the grab.'

I looked in the direction of the river, and saw that it was my friend from the Cambrian hills coming from the nearby boat-house.

'You might have a need of it,' he said, 'with the crackers that the children will be throwing for Guy Fawkes. Very dangerous they are for the thatch of the houses.'

So though it was but the first of the month, I shouldered the weapon. 'We use it on the river weeds,' he added. 'They'd choke the boat-house if we didn't act sharp with them.'

That night and for several nights after there was the crackle of musketry in the village as children let off their fireworks in the street and on the green. Then on the Fifth their parents went into action also, and bonfires blazed; rockets chased the crescent moon and did not catch it; stars broke in the sky and faded as they fell. The Great Bear and the Pole star remained unaffected; so did my thatch.

Next day I returned the trident to its place among the poplar twigs. You'd never know who might be wanting it as the moon grew to fullness.

CHAPTER THIRTY-THREE

'WHAT HAVE you got for the jumble sale?' called Major Talbot as, after standing in a north-east wind for half an hour in order to make a drawing of a few bullocks, I passed outside his gate.

'My tropical whites,' I said, with a shiver.

'When can I fetch them?' he asked.

This was serious. I had not expected to be taken literally.

'Let me think, let me search,' I said, hurrying on my way.

I felt like a bride about to pawn her wedding veil.

My whites, two of each and a pair of shorts, had been made for me in Maddox Street, W.1, just enough to get me to Fiji where, by Indian tailoring, price and quality would be on a lower level. How that double-breasted jacket was admired when I wore it at my first dinner-party in Suva! 'But won't you take it off?' asked my hostess, after fingering the lapels with admiration—it is etiquette in high-ranking Suva for male guests to arrive in a jacket, but to take it off almost at once at their hostess's suggestion.

I couldn't take it off because immediately under it I was wearing braces. Men living in the tropics tend to be lean, and a belt meets most requirements. But I started life overweight and have ever since exceeded it. Within the chaste doors of 45 Maddox Street I had suggested to Mr Manning (or Mr Pratt) that surely a

205

few bits of elastic would enable me to avoid shoulder harness.

'It is not that you are stout, sir,' said Mr Pratt (or Mr Manning) gracefully; 'it is just that your hips are too slight to support a belt.'

And now that jacket of which the Governor's wife in Apia had said to me: 'It is much too good for you to wear when you are with us,' was to be thrown to the jumblers.

Shrunk! Shrunk! All of them now unwearable by me. It really is fantastic how the best of materials, when put away in a drawer, can within a few years become reduced in measurement. Even leather, it seems, shrinks with time: I would not have believed it until in 1939 I tried on the Sam Browne belt which I had worn in 1914 and found a gape between tongue and buckle.

Is there any more romantic trousseau for a man than whites? As the rolls of shining twill are spread for his inspection, he senses the dazzle of sun-glazed walls and their reflections zigzagging deep into the dhow-studded waters, or the foam of iridescent waves singing and sighing on volcanic sands. Already a veil has fallen and as on a stage the scene has been transformed. When he walks out into the street again, colour has faded: even the flowers in shop windows and on barrows are drab as unlit coloured light bulbs. Only when eventually, by some unfocused process, he and his luggage have met in a cabin, and thence he has emerged on to an open deck, does an orchestra of gulls herald the raising of the curtain on another act. Then, whether he sleeps or wakes, waves curl at the bow, glisten as they pass, and sink into the immensity of the waters astern.   By day and by night the white furrow is churned, and smoothly as the soaring of the sea birds the ship moves on her course.   Dolphins curvet in merry greeting, a whale salutes with spume, and co-horts of silver-scaled wings speed a moment in the element of air to proclaim their warmer seas.

What lovelier times at sea than when tweeds have been folded and packed away—shorter twilights, brighter sunsets, and incandescent dawns.   The morn-ing bonfires throw from the east their jets of flame into cool filigrees of cloud: the midday sun lacquers the blue surface of the sea, and at evening tongues of madder and orpiment lick upwards towards the zenith. Then one day from the ship's rails we glimpse above the horizon a rim of hills, the boundary of a continent whose content of human life is hardly more known to us than that of the fishes beneath our keel.   Or it may be that hanging low over the horizon a solitary cloud tells of an islet beyond our view, an island of story-book romance or of the starkest tragedy.

'Ever heard of Clipperton Island?' asked Chief Engineer MacKail as, bound for Wellington, we left the Panama Canal behind us.   He and I were sitting on the starboard deck, waiting for the green flash—that moment when, after the red flare of the sun has sunk below the rim, one's eyes, dazzled, see only the complementary colour green.

'Called after Clipperton the pirate,' he said; 'made

it his hide-out for years.   About a thousand miles west of us now and right off the track.'

'Haven't I read of him somewhere?' I asked.

'In Dampier's voyages perhaps—he was his first mate till they quarrelled.'

'It was Dampier who put Crusoe ashore on Juan Fernandez,' I said.

'It was from a ship under his command that Selkirk went ashore of his own wish.   I know all about Selkirk—he was born at Largo, same as I was.   Largo in Fifeshire, in case you're ignorant—there's a fine bronze statue of him in the town.   We're an independent lot up there.   Selkirk ran away to sea in 1703. But he took against his captain, so stayed ashore on Juan Fernandez in 1704.'

'And lived to regret it?' I suggested.

'When Woodes Rogers came along four years later and took him on board his ship the *Duke*, and Crusoe saw that it was Dampier who was pilot, he was all for going back to his goats.'

'Why pilot?' I asked.   'I thought he was a captain.'

'So he had been, many times, but he couldn't command—always in trouble, falling foul of his officers and crew.   He died soon after that trip.   Clipperton was one of the officers that deserted him—he and about twenty men pinched a barque that they had taken as a prize off the coast of Mexico and hung out the Jolly Roger.'

The sun had set behind a low cloud—there was no green flash.   We moved to the after bar and sat on its veranda.

'And Clipperton Island?' I questioned, after Joe the steward had hastened to our help.

'An atoll, coral reef and lagoon, about five miles in circumference—not much use to anyone but Clipperton till a century ago,' said MacKail. 'At one time America thought it belonged to them, another time France, another time Mexico. Then some fellow out of his course found phosphate there—the only bit of high ground was guano. So a British firm sent out workers, and Mexico sent a few soldiers to retain authority, and every now and again a ship from Mexico would call with supplies. But when the First World War broke out the Mexicans forgot their garrison, and within three years the most of the hundred odd inhabitants were dead of starvation. So then the commander and what were left of his soldiers set off in an open boat and were never heard of again; and no sooner is their sail clear of the horizon than the keeper of the lighthouse, a giant of a Negro, comes along and murders the few men that remain and tries to take the women by force. But one of them catches him unawares and kills him with a hatchet; and would you believe it, the very next day an American ship turns up and takes off what was left—three women and a few kids.'

MacKail had a strong sense of humour but was incapable of laughing. When amused as he often was his face became florid and he would put his hand to his mouth, while his large body heaved and palpitated with emotion. That evening as he finished his tale of Clipperton Island, the purser joined us. He had a story for the chief.

'You know your namesake on the passenger list, Miss MacKail?' he said.

'No relation,' said the chief.

'Twenty years engaged, and now going to Australia to get married.'

'Canny,' commented the chief.

'This morning she had a cable from her fiancé. "The MacKails are coming, hurrah, hurrah!"'

'And what did she say to that?'

'She didn't say anything for a minute. Then: "*One* hurrah," she says, "would have been quite sufficient."'

The chief put his hand to his mouth as his face turned purple. His body shook and shivered as a New Zealand geyser does before it erupts. Then getting up as if about to have a convulsion, he hurried away, and I didn't see him again for two days. When next we met, at the same place, he produced a bit of paper with the three days' noon temperatures since we left Balbao.

'September 3rd, 84 degrees; 4th, 80 degrees; 5th, 74 degrees. We're crossing the line to-night,' he said. 'I told you it was cooler on the equator. The Humboldt current comes up from the south and strikes us here.'

Always some interest on board ship, whether over the side, over the masts, or in the small isolated community of which the one half travels in order to carry the other half upon its travels. Joe the steward was of the former. He was 'an institution.' Three days outward bound and he knew every passenger's requirements. His smile of welcome to the bar was as refreshing as a free drink. When as the weeks went by I took to dropping in during his less busy hours, he would confide to me details of his personal history.

'There was my father,' he said to me one day; 'he was seventy-five and the day he died he picked two winners. I went to see him and I said to him: "How are you, Dad?" And he says: "I'm happy, I picked two winners," and he died that night. Yes, and my Aunt Bella—she did love a thriller, a good murder one. She'd read one every night after she'd gone to bed, and then she'd finish up with a page from the *Pilgrim's Progress*. That was the one to put her to sleep quickest, she said.'

Another day when I found him in contemplative mood he spoke of his experiences as a prisoner of war.

'Queer how men change when they're inside,' he said. 'I was put in the bag in 1940, and there was fellows there who was taken with me, and for the first six months they talked about nothing but the good times they'd have when they got out—taking their wives to the pictures and the theatres, and giving them meals in posh restaurants. Then after a while they began to talk more about their homes—what they wished for was just to sit in their own arm-chairs with their wives beside them, and not move—not move an inch unless they wanted to. No one to order them to do anything, to wash themselves or to take exercise or go to bed. I was like that when I got back; all I asked was to sit and sit and say to myself that I was free. I wasn't married then—it didn't matter where I sat—but plenty of the boys had wives and it was hard on the

women.   They'd looked forward to a bit of life when
their men came home.'

A few days later in Long Wittenham post office one
of the stall holders at the jumble sale came up to me.
    'You'll be interested to hear,' she said, 'that Mrs
Lisbeck is going to make bolster cases out of the legs
of your white trousers, and her boy Benny says he can
make a sail for his canoe out of the seat.'
    But I hardly heard what she was saying, for I had just
received a letter from a friend in Nigeria inviting me
to join him there, and in my mind I was stepping
ashore at Lagos, clad in new and shining whites.

CHAPTER THIRTY-FOUR

I LIKE to be among the first to welcome a new landlord to a local pub. Is not the whole life of the community going to be affected, directly or indirectly, by that man's temperament?

'Grumpy and the whole village grumps, lordly and they puts on rockers,' as old Jack Buswell said to me. He had lived for many years at the other end of Berkshire, but had recently returned to his own village.

'There was Willie Ellis at the Three Bells, near where I been living,' he said; 'as nice a man as ever drawed a pint, could talk to anyone and genial to all, a proper family it was in there of a night. But—and I don't 'ardly like to say so—he had trouble with 'is wife. A bit too young and brittlesome she was. Then one night, 'bout an hour after closing time and a bright moon in the sky, parson comes along the road and hears a woman shouting, and he looks up and there's Mrs Willie half out of the window in her night-dress and Willie basting her. Well, mind you, I wouldn't say as she didn't deserve it, but parson wouldn't have it. "No," he says, "the church is trustee for this house and we can't 'ave it." Well, we was all right sorry when 'e went.

'Then along comes Harspole—*Mister* Harspole we called him. Never did like him. Mean! that man wouldn't give a name to his own dog—"Dog" was all he ever called him. You'd see the boys sittin' there glum of an evening after he came. I give up going.

213

Don't know what happened after 'cause I come back here to live.   Yes,' he said reflectively, 'the parson and the doctor is important on occasions, but for working days it's the man in the pub.   And I'll tell you another that's important to the village—the woman in the post. There's some of 'em wouldn't spare you the spit for a stamp, and there's others will write a letter for you.'

I had dropped in to welcome Mr Seary to the Vine, an old timbered house half way down the village street. Already everything was pursuing its course as prettily as the Windrush when it joins the Thames at Newbridge where Chris Seary had last hung his sign.   Out of doors there was a smell of frost in the air, but in the bar there was the comfort of a clear fire, with a great yellow cat sphinx-like before it.   Four young men, two of them in brightly coloured jerseys, were sitting round the table which stood in one of the corners opposite to the bar.   Tom Pender, a stout elderly man with a very red face, wearing a tweed hat and leather waist-coat, sat in the big arm-chair in the other corner. Two middle-aged men, one a stranger with a strong Welsh accent, were standing beside him.   In another arm-chair close to the fire sat old Jim Logsden, whose bright blue eyes shone in a grizzled face.   Getting on for eighty he was said to be.

The young men were arguing about coal.

'Of course it's mineral,' said one; 'it's carbon.'

'If it's made of ferns and trees, how can it be mineral?' demanded the other.

Old Jim by the fire looked up.   'I reckon a cow is flesh and bone,' he said, 'but she's made of grass.'

The conversation turned to pigs. Fred Dilley's Middle White sow had had thirteen piglets but she'd lain on one so as she wouldn't be bringing up an unlucky number. The Welshman said that on his farm in Breconshire he could tell the weather by his pigs' tails. 'The curl in them will straighten out before rain,' he said.

'Don't hold with that,' said Peter, his companion, a Wittenham man. 'If a pig's tail is straight he's in bad health, and if it twists round and round, kind of tight like, then he's got worms. A nice proper curl is what you want to see on a tail, then your pig's healthy.'

I told them of a pig in the West Indies who had been beaten because the people believed it had been bewitched, and next day an old woman had to be taken to hospital because of the wounds on her back.

'In Cardiganshire,' said the Welshman, 'they'll tell you of a hare that was shot in the leg but got away, and that evening an old woman, who lived in a cottage alone, was found near dead with her leg broken by a bullet.'

No one seemed inclined to believe these stories, so I told them of a pig that I'd known in the west of Ireland, who when it saw the devil on its owner's farm caught him by the tail and bit it. The pig's mouth was badly burned and its ears scorched before it loosed its hold, but the devil was so frightened that he took wing and was never seen in the district again. They didn't believe that either.

'What's that yarn of yours, Tom, 'bout the pig over at Uffington? Tell it to the landlord,' said one of the boys.

Tom lifted his hat, scratched his bald head and covered it again.

''Twas my mother used to tell of a couple lived over in Uffington, near the White Horse,' he said.   'Farm workers they were with a bit of a garden and some hens and a pig.   'Twas a big occasion when the pig was killed—chitterlings, fry, griskin, sperrib, and all the rest of it.   One time, the day after they'd killed, George—that was the husband—he had some for his breakfast; he had some for his dinner, he had some for his tea, and he had some for his supper.   And then in the night Emily—that was his wife—she woke up and found him pullin' on his trousers.

'"What be at, Garge, whur be gwine?" she says.

'"Oi be gwine down to 'ev some mohre uv that peg. Be you gwine to 'ev some?"

'"Naw, thet Oi byeant."

'"Then you bide thur an stahve i' the land o' plenty. Oi be gwine to 'ev some," he said.   And he did.'

'Don't know much about pigs; it's sheep I reckon is good weather prophets,' said Chris Seary, who was a Berkshire man.   'See 'em scattered all about the field and it'll be fine; see 'em all hunched together and there'll be a storm.'

'When it's wet mucky weather they lamb quicker. When it's dry barren, they 'ang on and on,' said Tom.

The door opened and a slight figure in breeches and leggings came in.

'Here's Lionel, he'll tell you about cattle,' said Jim.

'What about cattle?' asked Lionel.

'Does they tell the weather?'

'It affects 'em,' said Lionel.

'How affects 'em?'

'Well, twentieth of the month to-day.   Yesterday I go up to have a look at a heifer due to calve the thirtieth. No sign o' calving.   This morning herdsman comes in. ''That heifer's calved,'' he says.   Foggy night, came down thick, that's what brought her on.'

'Have you known it happen before?' I asked.

'Same thing last year,' he said, 'with three heifers I'd bought.   They wasn't due to calve for a fortnight, but one evening when I been up in the meadow to see to them the fog come down that heavy I had to follow the wire of the fence with me hand to get home—when I felt four strands I knew I was near the gate.   Next morning there was three calves in the field.'

After a pause while glasses were filled, old Jim looked across at Tom.   'Got your broad beans in yet?' he asked.

'Putting 'em in to-morrow,' said Tom.

'That's right, before Advent Sunday.   ''When parson reads from end of Book, it's time to sow broad beans.''   Rules by the Bible can't be beat, same as puttin' in the taters on Good Friday.'

'Haven't bought me seed beans yet,' murmured one of the younger men.

'Never bought a bean in me life,' said old Jim. 'When first I started gardening, my father he give me a handful o' beans.   ''That's good stock,'' he said, ''the same as I started with when I were a lad, and I saved the seed every year since.''   And every year I done the same, and I'll be seventy-six next week.   I puts in the beans one between each o' my spring cabbages, that gives 'em shelter from the frosts. It was my father give me my first runners, too. Seven beans he give me and I planted 'em beside the door, and I never picked a bean from them that first year, left 'em all for seed.'

'And I'll tell you,' said Tom, 'how I keep mine from the rooks. Each year when it's sowing time I makes a drill and I puts holes in it, and then I walks along it bending down as if I was putting a bean in each hole, and then I rakes it over and I leaves it. And all the time the rooks is watchin' me, and first light next mornin' they's down looking for those beans and o' course they can't find 'em because they isn't there. So that same day then I goes along and makes holes again and pretends I'm putting in beans, and I rakes it over careful and I leaves it, and next mornin' the rooks is there again digging and o' course they can't find none. And I does the same again on the third day. So then the rooks says to themselves, "He's a silly old coot, he is, he's not putting in beans at all," so when I *does* put 'em in on the fourth day they doesn't bother to come into the garden.'

'How's the flower garden been?' I asked Jim, for I remembered its brightness in other years.

'None too good; never been the same, not since she died. No one to argue with nowadays—it makes a difference in a garden; no one to argue with now 'cept the snails. She was a great one for the flowers, my wife—liked seeing them agrowing. She never wanted to have them in the house, but she liked to walk in the

garden and look at them.   And she knew all their
names too—many a time I asked her when I couldn't
remember meself what something was called, and she
always knew.   Yes, I miss her.   I've lived alone now
near eleven years—no one to argue with me, only the
snails.'

'What do they say to you?' asked Tom.

''Twas only a few weeks back I came on a bunch of
them in a hole in the greenhouse wall,' said Jim.   'I
didn't smash 'em because she didn't like me to do that.
But I had a pot of paint in me hand 'cause I was painting
the frames, and with me finger I put a dab of white on
every shell.   So as I'll know you if ever I sees you
again, I explained to them.   Then I threw 'em over the
garden wall into the meadow, as far as I could throw.
Would you believe it—sure as a swallow the most of
them was back on the greenhouse next morning.'

CHAPTER THIRTY-FIVE

WHEN YOU'VE walked the two miles of towpath down-stream from Shifford and passed through the small grey Thames Conservancy gate marked T.C. 50, you need go no further, for already you are on the lawn of the Maybush at Newbridge and doors are open to welcome you. On one side of the house are the six pointed arches of the medieval bridge that spans not only the Thames but its tributary the Windrush almost at their junction; on the other side are the seven rounded and more recent flood arches that carry away rising waters. You might be in a ship at sea in that house, for from every window you look out on to moving water, and day and night you hear the gurgling of the stream as it divides at the massive buttresses.

'If that bridge was built in eleven hundred and something, why is it called Newbridge?' asked a visitor.

'Because,' said the local historian, 'there was another bridge there before it.'

The same historian records that during a period of

economic depression earlier in the century two elderly
bachelors of the neighbourhood decided to go to
America.   Plenty of work over there, plenty of wages,
and every man welcome, was what they had heard.

'But how do we go there?' asked Bert, the younger.

'Why, in a boat, of course,' said George, the elder.

So without saying where they were going they
borrowed a fishing-punt, and with the little they had of
possessions they set off down-stream.   After a couple
of miles they came to Northmoor and six miles after
that they came to Eynsham where because they passed
under instead of over the bridge no toll was demanded
of them, and then with the wind behind them they
reached Abingdon.   But overnight the wind turned
against them and it was two hard days' rowing before
they sighted Reading.   That night George said to Bert:
'I've had enough of this voyaging,' he said.   'You're
young,' he said, 'and you may go on to America if you
like, but I'm going back to England.'

When I last called at the Maybush it was late in
January.   The sky was leaden grey and tongues of
bitter wind licked at the opaque water; but towards
evening the gusts abated and died away, the clouds
dissolved and bands of pale amber vapour spread across
a leaf-green western sky.   Thorn thickets by the
Windrush turned livid and the now calm water mirrored
their redness, deeply.   The distant willows stood
against the evening light like frail purple coral fans.
As I wandered over the flat-breasted water meadows,
thinking mostly of the moles in their shallow runs and
what they would do when the river rose after the

week's rain, and casting an occasional thought to the fish that threw silent teasing circles on the surface of the river, I saw shining on the bank a small pile of fish scales and from it to the water's edge the track of an

otter. Where the animal had come ashore, and with the fish in its mouth had climbed on to the grass, the footprints were deep and clearly marked in the mud; but where after its meal it had returned to the water, the track was hardly more than a series of long slithers.

That evening in the bar I mentioned what I had seen.

'I know that animal,' said one of the regulars. 'Up there many an evening I seen him scouring the river. You don't hear much flopping of the fish when he's about.'

I asked if there were many otters in those waters.

'Plenty of 'em moving about; you hear 'em whistling to each other o' nights. 'Course, they don't stay long in one place, though I reckon there's a pair got their holt in the bank below Badger Wood. By an old willow-tree up by the second gate, at the bend of the river—you can't see the opening 'cause it's under the water among the roots, but I seen the cubs playing on the bank above like a couple of pups.'

'And badgers?' I asked.

'Plenty of them too. You'll see the setts all over the hill behind the little spinney.'

A man who was leaning against the bar turned to me.

'I suppose you've met Sunny by this?' he asked.

'Sunny, the big yellow cat that Chris took with him to Wittenham?'

'You'd think that cat was the new landlord at the Vine,' I said, 'the way it owns the place.'

'Has Chris told you about him and the Labrador?'

'Not yet,' I said.

'Chris had that cat for years, and the two of them was that close that Chris could hardly draw a pint of beer without the cat on his shoulder. Daft, we used to say, and Chris would laugh, and you'd swear the cat was laughing too. Then someone gave Chris a dog, a Labrador, a fine black Labrador, and the cat went mad jealous, spitting and snarling and ready with its claws at every moment of the day. "You'll have to get rid of one of them," we used to tell him. Well, you'd be scared to sit in the bar with that cat if the dog showed his nose at the window or the door. And so it went on all the winter. "You'll lose trade," we said to Chris; "people don't like cats spitting in their beer," we said.

'And then one night, end of January when the floods was up, just before closing time Chris puts the cat outside the door for a few minutes same as he always did at that time. Such a night—as bad as I ever remember and the house like an island with the floods. Well, he was hardly back behind the bar to serve us a last round when we heard a screech that would frighten you—a badger's screech it was, and a minute later there was another. Did you ever hear a badger screech? Like six cats, only louder. So Chris rushes out to see what's happened and the wind bangs the door and we all sits there waiting for him to come back.

And then he comes in with the cat in his arms, flat out
the animal was—dead, we thought.   And Mrs Chris
sits down and takes it on her lap, and there was a lump
on its head like a hen's egg, and its coat was torn and
thick with mud.   No, it wasn't bitten—badgers only
fights with their claws.   And when anybody touched it,
it shivered—proper hurt it was.   And then in comes
the big Labrador from the kitchen, and it goes up to the
cat and it starts licking it—licks it all over, and
presently the cat opens its eyes and sees the dog, and it
never moves.   And the dog goes on licking and licking,
kind of comforting.   And do you know from that
instant moment those two animals was friends—bosom
friends, you might call 'em.   They'd sleep together o'
nights, and if in the daytime the dog was shut inside the
kennel the cat would climb up and lie on top of the
wire just to be near him.'

When a few days later I returned to Wittenham and
called at the Vine with greetings from old friends at
Newbridge, alterations had begun and I found a chaos

of wattle, daub and old timbers in the garden, and indoors cavities in almost every wall.   The staircase had disappeared completely and, looking up the now vacant shaft, I saw doors standing open, empty and gruesome as eye sockets.   But everyone was cheerful, not least the three builders who were eating their sandwich lunches in the bar.   Two of them were of normal dimensions; the third was enormous, and though Peter was his name he was known to all as Paddy.

'Tipperary I come from,' he said.

'And I'm from Cork—just sixty-four and a half miles from Cashel,' I said.

'When were you last in County Tipp?' he asked.

'Fifty years ago,' I told him.

'And aren't you smart to be remembering the distance.'

'If you'd travelled those miles on a bicycle before breakfast, you'd remember them,' I said.

'Over the mountains too, the Knockmealdowns, and they didn't have tarred roads in those days,' he said.

'No,' I answered, 'but they had an east wind that blew in my face whichever way I travelled.'

'What put you on the road at that time of day?'

So then I told him how, because of a kind of wager with a friend of my father's who had been made Dean of Cashel and whom I had often visited for breakfast when his parish was but twenty miles away, I set out on my bicycle one midnight, thinking the distance to be no more than forty miles at most.   Why I chose that particular night I don't know, except that it was some special Sunday, and after long sittings in church my legs had grown stiff.   I was wanting to stretch them when, during the last sermon of the day, I remembered that Bob Creber the sexton was courting a girl at Rathcormac, which would be half way on the road to Cashel.

'Will you come with me, Bob?' I asked after I had told him of my project and he was locking the gate of the churchyard.

'I will, Master Bob,' he said; 'will I call for you?'

'I'll call for you,' I said, 'at midnight.'

This companion of mine was a man of distinction. Not only could he climb the tallest and barest tree without artificial aid, but when at the top and swaying on the tenderest of branches he could sing a hymn or, if his audience preferred it, his favourite song, 'Martha whacked the donkey,' which for its full rendition needed action that would make a Derby jockey in his saddle seem limp in comparison.   Bob was a perfect sexton, sitting far back in the church and leading the responses.   Only once on each alternate Sunday did his voice fail, and that after the clause in the Litany which concerned 'all the nobility.'   The congregation had to say the 'We beseech Thee' on their own, for Bob saw no reason why exalted people should have a special prayer.   Hadn't they already got all they wanted and more than they needed in this world?

And so we set off, each of us with his little oil-lamp glimmering below the handle-bars.   Along the straight road into Cork and through the city's deserted streets, and away down by the estuary of the Lee, with the tide out and aromatic whiffs coming up the harbour with the east wind.   Of course at such an hour in the morning that wind wouldn't have risen enough to be noticeable if we hadn't been working against it. It was there right enough even as on foot we pushed our machines up the rough mountainy road towards Fermoy.

At Rathcormac Creber left me, with a doubt in his heart, I felt, of the welcome he'd be getting from his prospective father-in-law an hour before daybreak. With the longer half of my journey ahead, I faced towards the Kilworth and Galtee mountains. The cool sweet smell of dawn was in the air, and the misty light that comes from nowhere was spreading above the hill-bound road. I do not remember much more except that a hobbled donkey half asleep on the side of the road gave me a look as I passed, as if to say 'Up early!' and that half a mile beyond I saw a man moving behind a cottage which might have been a heather-thatched boulder and had the same thought myself about him.

The last few flat miles towards that rock set on a hill, whose cluster of twelfth-century ecclesiastical buildings is among the most impressive in Great Britain or Ireland, were the final destruction of my thigh muscles. I could no longer push down the pedals, I could only lean against the saddle and drag my feet after it. It was twenty minutes to nine when I staggered through the deanery gate, in time for breakfast.

The war whoop that the dean let out when he saw me on the path would have silenced the Angel Gabriel. Apart from my father, that man was the loveliest cleric I've ever known: a bald head, big bags under his star-like eyes, large ears that he could waggle at will, and a laugh that was like the bells of heaven.

CHAPTER THIRTY-SIX

I T W A S the morning after I had hauled my boat on to the river-bank and spent the afternoon bending over it, fitting new floorboards, that the pains of lumbago gripped me. Not for fifteen years had I been so afflicted. Then a Wise Man in Wales had cured me by working a spell with a bit of knitting wool; but I knew of no such wisdom in Wittenham. So, painfully, I picked my steps down the rough gravelled path to my studio, and I reached the Chippendale chair, with arms and beauty but no great comfort, in which as a boy while reading Gray's *Anatomy* of the internal regions I had dreamt of surface anatomy at the Slade.

'Never to rise again,' I thought, as, with only the upper half of my own anatomy capable of action, I bravely took up a pencil, gave it a run in my turn-the-wheel sharpener, and settled down to think.

There wasn't a scratch on the paper before me when I heard a scratch on the door. The damn pup. Quietly, with not a sound, not even of a pencil thinking, I sat. One excuse is as good as another when you have no ideas. And then there came another scratch, and a squeak, and a small bark.

What could I do but rise up, stagger across, and let her in. Such a greeting—ears flapping, legs galloping. Up with the old woolly slipper, her favourite toy; down with the old woolly slipper and up with a stick of firewood; then down with the firewood and round and round the studio with a chunk of coal.

By this time I had creaked back to my chair—the chair with the clawed arms that my grandfather had given to my mother and that now had a seat upholstered with stitchery by my sister; and I was sitting, half leaning for support, at my writing-table with its bit of Kerry homespun that serves as a covering, when there was a bark at my feet.

'Quiet!' I said.

Another bark and a pull at my trousers.

'Quiet!' I said again, with more emphasis.

'Gr-r-r-r!' and a bite that pierced my slipper.

'Stop it!' I said crossly, pushing her away with what strength I had in my legs.

'Gr-r-r-r!' and another tug at the turn-up of my trousers.

Painfully I turned in my chair. 'Out of it!' I said fiercely. But all she did was to dance and prance about my feet, biting at everything, including my admonishing hand.

'Out of it—stop!' I shouted again, lifting my left foot and trying to kick with my right. 'Out of it!' I repeated, as I raised my right foot and tried to kick with my left. She dodged between the legs of my chair, pulled at the fringe of the homespun as she passed and came back to the attack laughing. But for acrobatic action on my part, pens, pencils, papers, and paste-pot would have been on the floor. This time she caught me astern by the pullover, and I could scarcely twist an inch to free myself.

Then from the house came the clear accented call: 'Lunch is ready!'

Tai-lua dropped her grip and ran to the door. Stiffly I rose and followed her. To my surprise the gravel on the path outside seemed less boulderous than it had been earlier. Tai pulled at my trousers so that from a walk I had to break into a hobbling trot. At the end of the path she took the three steps in one bound; I followed in two.

'You *have* made a quick recovery,' I was greeted at the door.

And so I had.

CHAPTER THIRTY-SEVEN

Y O HO ! The floods are out, and the valley is
a sky-reflecting lake with only a murky turbu-
lence to mark the course of the river. On
either side of the current clear quiet waters
seep gently among the spring grasses.

'Marvellous—a world of silver!' I said to a woman
who came and stood beside me on Clifton Bridge.

'It'll be a marvel,' said she, 'if it doesn't come in
under my door—only four inches to go now. We've
rolled up the carpet and moved all the furniture
upstairs.'

I thought of a time when, staying at the Hotel
Monaco in Venice, the proprietor had asked me if I
would mind for the same reason moving to a higher
level in the bar. Even St Mark in his own square had
been unable to control the combined effects of high
tides and strong winds: the piazza was deep under
water, and the ground floors of most buildings in the
city were awash. Here beside the Thames, to escape
the rising waters snails had climbed reed stems and
slugs had climbed trees. Wrens, driven from their
lowly habitats of hedge and scrub, were bustling from
trunks to boles of willows. Never did I see so many
wrens—there seemed to be one to every tree. And
from the quiet waters that spread over emerald fields,
pooling them with lavender, there emerged dead
branches inert and gnarled as crocodiles. Where a few
logs lay one upon another above flood level, partridges

took cover.   Under my boat, pulled high, a field-mouse sheltered.

In the boat I could row unhindered over hedges and boundary fences, taking them as lightly as a hunter at a horse show.   Into the water garden, through whose tall reeds I had first walked to find the river, I sailed as though I were part of a Japanese painting on pale shimmering silk.   Above me on their latticed stems the mist-grey plumes fluttered; below me their reflections sank into the trembling water.   Where nearer to the river's course the current scoured its way, a weeping willow trailed golden hair.

And soon throughout the valley where those waters swirled, hazel catkins would be streaming in the wind, hawthorn hedges would be flushed with green, and new-born lambs would leap in lush grass patched with celandines and daisies.

Some men crave islands, some crave mountain tops: it is water that calls to me.   Fresh or salt, tranquil in a pool or thunderous on a shore, lapping at bent grasses or leaping from a prow, the insistence is the same. Psychologists may know the reason—I am content with the appetite.

Not long ago, when I was coming home by train from London, a stranger sitting in the opposite seat of the compartment spoke to me as we neared our destination.

'I think you must be the author of *Sweet Thames Run Softly*,' he said.

'How did you know?' I asked.

'Because every time we crossed the river or passed near it, you leaned forward to look out,' he answered.

He might indeed have mentioned also the tributaries and many a water- and bird-filled gravel-pit along the line. The canal and sand-pits at West Drayton, the River Loddon twice at Twyford; the Thames at Maidenhead, Reading, Pangbourne, and again at Tile-hurst, Goring, and Moulsford: I watch for them all.

But it isn't only the Thames and its attendant brooks that bring my nose to the carriage window. Wherever I may be travelling, I rarely read lest by so doing I miss a glimpse of river, duck pond, or canal. Even if I buy papers, serious and light, before taking my seat, they serve only to pass the time until the train starts. At the first whistle from the guard, leading ladies find themselves face to face with leading editorials on the rack above my head.

There is nothing unusual in this love of water. Poets throughout the ages have sung of the peace of gently running streams. In the sacred writings a river is used constantly as a symbol of peace: 'Then had thy peace been as a river,' 'He leadeth me beside the still waters.' Throughout our own literature flows the timeless tranquillity of rivers. Spenser's *Pro-thalamion* is borne on the waters of Sweete Themmes. The tortured mind of Swift longed for a river at his garden's end. The gentler Stevenson wished to all 'a living river by the door.' I think it is the unbroken sequences of flowing water, the unchanging destinies of streams, that seem to knit a man's soul with the eternities. The rhythms of eddying pools, the rhymes of lapping wavelets, bring peace through eye and ear, emphasizing by their unceasing flow the unimportance

of our passing lives.   On and on they glide, not merely
for the brief moments of our attention but through
every hour of night and day, varying yet constant.
The dancing of a mountain stream
may be as entrancing as a ballet, but
the quiet of an age-old river is like
the slow turning of pages in a well-
loved book.

Sweete Themmes! runne softly, till I end my Song.